MEET THE FAB FIVE

John and Nick, neighborhood pals from industrial Birmingham, who threw in their lot together to form a band . . .

Gorgeous Simon, drama school student, who discovered his best role as Duran Duran's lead singer . . .

Andy, who taught himself to play the guitar at five, and strummed his way into the hearts of millions at twenty-one . . .

Adorable Roger, who shocked friends and family by turning down a career in the auto industry in favor of banging on drums . . .

HERE IS THE BEHIND-THE-SCENES STORY OF THE HOTTEST BAND OF THE DECADE—AND AN INTIMATE GLIMPSE INTO THE PRIVATE LIVES OF THE FIVE SUPERSTARS WHO ARE . . . DURAN DURAN!

TRIVIA MANIA
by Xavier Einstein

TRIVIA MANIA has arrived! With enough questions to answer every trivia buff's dreams, TRIVIA MANIA covers it all—from the delightfully obscure to the seemingly obvious. Tickle your fancy, and test your memory!

DURAN DURAN

By Cynthia C. Kent

ZEBRA BOOKS
KENSINGTON PUBLISHING CORP.

Cover Photo by John Bellissimo

ZEBRA BOOKS

are published by

Kensington Publishing Corp.
475 Park Avenue South
New York, N.Y. 10016

First printing: August 1984

Printed in the United States of America

DURAN DURAN

CONTENTS

1. Duran Duran: Live

It's the night before the box office opens. Already there are at least thirty people on line. Most of them are young—anywhere from fifteen to eighteen. The younger kids wanted to be here, but their parents wouldn't let them come. They sent their older brothers and sisters. Some have sleeping bags, others have chairs. They are here for the night. Tickets go on sale at nine o'clock and they are going to get them no matter how long they have to wait or how much it costs.

It's an event that happens maybe once a year: their favorite group Duran Duran has finally come to town! Tickets for any of their concerts are a scarce commodity. Some of the people on this rapidly increasing line have been to a Duran Duran concert before, others have not. The ones who have had the supreme pleasure of seeing the "Fab Five" perform eagerly tell those less fortunate just what they can expect. A Duran Duran concert is an intense celebration. The fans that will gather are devout followers of the group. They will sing along with every song. Dancing in the aisles is almost mandatory. The group will perform all the biggest hits including "Hungry Like the Wolf," "Girls on Film," and "Rio."

The fans on line begin to develop a warm friendship. None of them have ever met before, but their mutual admiration and devotion to Duran Duran makes conversation open and easy. "My favorite album is *Rio*," says one girl who has become involved in conversation with the group in front of her. "Yeah, I really liked *Rio*, but I think *Seven and the Ragged Tiger* is really *great*! I love 'The Reflex,' it's such a great song," adds another. "Who's your favorite?" "I really can't decide, I think I love John, but Roger is so cute and so shy." "Oh, God, I hope we get tickets, I can't wait!"

The box office opens in the morning, bright and early. They'll be ready.

"I've got two!" an excited teenager tells her best friend over the phone. "You did? I'm so jealous! Who are you taking?" the friend replies, anxiously awaiting her answer. "Oh, I don't know . . . ummm, you wanna go?" "Yes, yes, yes!" They'll be there.

It's the night before the long-awaited concert. Those lucky people who have tickets are in a state of panic. Most feel they'll probably die before the day of the concert finally arrives. They prepare for the event by listening to all their Duran Duran albums over and over again, memorizing the lyrics, and hoping the band will play their favorite song. Many spend the evening watching MTV, waiting for one of Duran Duran's famous videos to be aired. Those fortunate enough to own a copy of the Duran Duran video LP pop it into the VCR and watch it over and over again, getting psyched for tomorrow's spectacular concert. Many preparations have to be made. Who will buy the flowers? Everyone wants to bring elaborate bouquets to the concert to present to the band backstage—if they are lucky enough to get backstage—or just to toss up on stage during the performance. Who'll drive to the arena? Where will everyone go afterwards to rave about the concert and fill each other in on their

11

favorite parts? The most frequently asked question is "What are you going to wear?" Many will decide on safari outfits that mimic the costumes of the now-famous video "Hungry Like the Wolf." Others will be less creative, but all will wear enough "I love Duran Duran" buttons to risk wounding themselves if they fall. One thing is certain: All will have a sensational time.

"What is *with* you tonight? You haven't been listening to a word I'm saying!"

"Oh, Mom! How can you expect me to think about anything but the concert? It's only nineteen more hours!"

"For God's sake it's only a concert."

"But it's *Duran Duran*."

"It's what?"

"That's the name of the band, Mom. Duran Duran. See that poster behind you? That's them."

"Which one is Duran?"

"Oh, Mom!"

"Is it this one?"

"That's Simon. There is no Duran. That's just the name of the band. Simon's OK, but my favorite is Roger on the right."

"I think Simon is cuter."

"Oh, Mom!"

Nick Rhodes and John Taylor are backstage in a cramped, bare waiting room. They nervously puff cigarettes as they discuss the lineup for the show they are about to perform. "Let's begin with 'Rio,' " says John, "then move into 'Save a Prayer' and 'New Moon on Monday.' " Nick agrees to this. This concert is very important. He remembers the early days of Duran Duran, when he and John would sit around talking about fictional concert dates. "Hammersmith Odeon by 1982," they would say, "Madison Square Garden by 1983, and world domination by 1984!" They were doing more than dreaming, they were carefully planning. And now they are about to play Madison Square Garden with world domination just around the corner.

The rest of the band, Andy, Roger and Simon, join Nick and John in the backstage room. As Andy stamps out his cigarette and Roger takes a last sip of his soda, a stage hand sticks his head in and informs them that it's time. Simon does a funny, bouncy dance step on his toes, points toward the door and with his fist raised in the air and shouts, "Rock & roll!"

Duran Duran heads for the stage.

This twenty thousand seat arena is SRO tonight. The great stage, full of amps, guitars, wires, speakers and other sound equipment, is

13

barely lit now, but soon it will be ablaze with an array of colored lights, action and music. The crowd is buzzing with a tense, but glorious anticipation. In the properly designated seats, photographers—some of the rock world's best and most famous—are perched upon their chairs, Nikons in hand, ready to focus, flash, and freeze on film the band they've come to see. They are ready to capture the intensity, the excitement, the glamour.

Suddenly, as the house lights go down and the stage lights come up, a voice is heard over the powerful P.A.: "Ladies and gentlemen, Madison Square Garden is proud to introduce Duran Duran!" A blond, modellike Simon Le Bon approaches the microphone; clad in leather pants, a lean John Taylor picks up his bass; Andy Taylor, dark glasses intact, takes his guitar; shy Roger Taylor slides smoothly behind his drums; an androgenous Nick Rhodes casually and anxiously fingers his keyboard. As the band takes the stage the fast-rising roar of the audience reaches a decibel level almost unbearable—a roar that has been described as a "million insects rubbing their legs together." These are the joyful screams of the same fans who waited in those seemingly endless box office and Ticketron lines to pay any price just to be here tonight. The same fans who bought all of the now-famous Duran Duran LPs, putting this band from Britain at the very top of the rock and pop charts. The fans who watched this "Fab Five", as they have come to be labeled, in some of the most sizzling videos ever to be transmitted through a cable wire. In short, the fans who adore them.

As the excited howling reduces to a dull hum, the band breaks into one of their many hits:

> Shake up the picture the lizard mixture
> With the dance on the eventide
> You got me coming up with answers
> All of which I deny *
> > "New Moon On Monday"
> > From *Seven and the Ragged Tiger*

With every word, lead singer Simon Le Bon tugs at the heartstrings of every young female fan present. His special phrasing, emotional delivery and quirky dancing is stamped with that Duran Duran quality that has made the band what they are today: rock & roll superstars.

*Words and Music by Duran Duran Copyright 1983 Tritec Music

Only about five years ago Duran Duran were a couple of young guys hacking around a few clubs in Birmingham with a guitar and a synth box with dreams of stardom. Today, they are the forerunners of the most recent British invasion in the world of rock & roll. This 1984 Madison Square Garden gig was the culmination of their rapid-fire success story. A packed house in one of the largest arenas in North America solidified Duran Duran's position as the international rock phenomenon of the decade. This was New York, but it could have been just about anywhere in the world. Canada, Japan, England, Australia—not a thing would have been different. Because after three multimillion-seller LPs and at least nine top ten singles, Duran Duran has taken the world by storm.

Duran Duran's first American tour took place in 1981, following the smash success of their first single record, "Planet Earth." Although the first tour did not exactly make them superstars with American audiences, the band returned to these shores in 1982 for a second tour, after the success of their debut LP in Britain and Australia. That time, the fan reaction to these five handsome golden boys of pop-rock music was nothing short of phenomenal. Then, in 1984, Duran Duran returned to the road after two additional albums dominated the record charts: *Rio* and *Seven and the Ragged Tiger*. (Both *Rio* and their latest LP, *Seven and the Ragged Tiger*, have attained platinum status; their debut LP, *Duran Duran*, has gone gold and is still selling.) Once again they swept this country and many others with a pop hysteria not witnessed since the Beatles toured the States in 1964.

Their music has been labeled "night music" for its delicate phrasing, radical lyrics (as Simon calls them), unique melodies and that electro-funk beat that has had the club scene vibrating since the band surfaced in 1978. They have been called "the band made in videoland," owing their sudden popularity (in the States especially, it was almost instantaneous) to their video "Hungry Like the Wolf"—which featured the five sexy Britons traipsing through the exotic jungles of Sri Lanka. The excellently crafted video clip immediately caught and held the attention of the MTV audience. It was different. It stood out; they stood out. The cable viewers hungered for more. And they descended upon record stores to buy Duran Duran's music.

But the band had their own ideas about this sudden popularity. "It was frightening at the beginning," said bass player John Taylor. "It

17

sort of took us by surprise, because we were the first group in years and years that have had it—thousands of kids running after the limousines. We've had to park the car and have dummy limousines go to the theaters all over Britain, Japan, even places like Portugal and Sweden."

During their first world tour, thousands of fans waited outside concert halls just to catch a glimpse of one of the Durans. In the typical fanaticism that often overtakes the rock fan, many went so far as to invade the hotels where the band and their crew were staying. Some even managed to call certain members of the band at home. As Nick Rhodes commented: "It got to the point where we couldn't eat—we were trapped." But he added: "The fans are very loving though, they are always sending us presents."

Fan hysteria has become an expected reaction to any Duran Duran concert. In some ways the band loves it. As John Taylor said, "Sometimes I think girls yell at concerts because they're out on the town and away from their parents and we give them good music and great smiles." There is certainly no arguing the fact that girls can really shout at a Duran Duran concert. Much like the Beatles, Duran Duran is conducting a U.S. tour that no one can really hear.

18

For a little more about Duran Duran and just what it is about them that makes women swoon in America and across the world, let's take a closer look. . . .

2. Presenting Duran Duran

How an entertainer presents himself to his audience determines how successful he will be. The public, after all is said and done, is the most difficult hurdle to surmount on the road to stardom. A singer's voice may be wonderful, or a songwriter's talents incredible, but the entertainer's image ultimately is what wins over the audience. With the entertainment world as difficult a nut to crack as it is, it takes more these days to become a star than talent. It takes charm, beauty, personality and uniqueness. An artist that lacks these qualities may find his career over before it's really started.

Most of the rock world's most successful artists have been those with powerful and honest images. A fine example of this in the 1980s is singer Cyndi Lauper, whose debut LP, *She's So Unusual*, describes Ms. Lauper to a tee. Cyndi is unusual—different—but at all times very much herself. Her fashion and appearance are not the result of some record company make-over; her music is very much her own style. And it's very apparent that Cyndi really believes in what she's doing. This comes across in her live performances as well as her recordings.

David Bowie (who has had a strong influence on Duran Duran) is another artist whose image has always been a vital selling point during his triumphant career. Throughout the years, Bowie has created a series of different and fascinating characters through which his music flowed as the lines of a play flow through the actors on stage. Much thought and innovation went into characters like Ziggy Stardust.

Culture Club's phenomenal success has everything to do with Boy George's image. Certainly, the music of Culture Club would not sound a bit different if Boy George wore a suit and tie instead of his usual flamboyant garb. But the fact that Boy George offers his audience an alternative image, showing the world that he's not afraid to be himself and do what he believes in has made him a worldwide super-star.

Duran Duran shares something very important with these other performers in style, image and ideology. All of these artists, and especially Duran Duran, are determined to promote individuality through their music. What each of these celebrities is saying to the world when they don unusual clothes and outrageous makeup is that being yourself, doing what feels good and natural to you, is all that matters. These artists are accepted by their fans for who and what they choose to be.

Duran Duran has encouraged self-confidence and individual expression from the very start of their career. What they wanted to get across to their fans was a positive point of view: confidence in yourself and your own ambitions were the most important things in life. And that kind of thinking made all their dreams come true.

Yet the Durans feel that they are no different from anyone else. They worked hard and fought hard to realize their ultimate goal. Their message is, "If we can do it, so can you." Whether you want to be a pop star, or a train driver, don't ever give up your dreams. "What we're trying to offer," lead singer Simon Le Bon says, "is an alternative point of view which says, 'So everything is going wrong, but don't just sit there and moan about it—if anything is going to happen, it's only because it's you that's going to make it happen, you as an individual, doing what you have to do."

Bassist John Taylor echoed that sentiment when he told a reporter recently, "Basically speaking, if you've got something on your mind, you shouldn't give up until you get it. And that's true of anything, not just music."

An attitude like that is contagious. It's more than contagious, it's overwhelming. It's been a major factor in Duran Duran's success and their enormous appeal. Literally millions of pop-loving fans are applying that attitude to their own lives. More and more people are catching the Duran Duran fever every day. In a world that is so difficult to live in (especially for young people)—with governments collapsing, wars flaring up, corruption and crime—a group as idealistic as Duran Duran is like a breath of fresh air.

Two other factors that are important elements of the Duran Duran image are of course their physical appearance and the light, melodic and unpolitical quality of their music. The Durans are wonderfully handsome—no doubt about it—and they do everything they can to maintain those gorgeous faces and physiques. But as hard as it is to believe, the band has actually been criticized for looking good.

Some people conclude that the only reason a fan becomes interested in Duran Duran is because she's young and female and she likes to look at gorgeous men. This is unfair. It may be a consideration at first, but only when a potential fan listens to that sweetly melodic music and catches on to the dazzling electro-funk beat, is he or she hooked for good. And it's really not only the teenage females that love Duran Duran. When a band is selling three million records a year, you can be sure that people of all ages and tastes are buying them. The bottom line of the Duran Duran image and appeal is that the band is simply great.

Duran Duran was the victim of other unfair judgments during the initial stages of their career. The narrow-minded press called them "strictly a business entity," claiming that their music was bland and that they were using their good looks to reach a particular record-buying audience simply in order to earn a great deal of money. This has been the most difficult criticism for the band to shake. True, a great deal of money has been made by the band and their managers and record company. And a great deal of money had been spent to promote the group. Of course they are millionaires, but no one can deny that they have worked extremely hard to earn their keep. The issue for Duran Duran is: How good a product can we produce? Yes, they do produce elaborate and expensive videos. Yes, they do record in large, state-of-the-art recording studios with expensive production work. But this is not because Duran Duran are mercenary businessmen, but only because they want to produce the finest quality they are capable of—videos and records that are unique and new, work that they truly can be proud of. Money is not what's important—being creative and reaching as many people as possible with their music is all Duran Duran have ever wanted to do. Fortunately their wealth has finally put them in a position to be able to do that.

Duran Duran deliver everything a fan could ask for. Great videos, great dancing music, and great stage shows. Performing is what the Durans love to do most—these guys believe in putting on a show! On their most recent tour they put on their flashiest show ever: extra musicians, tons and tons of lights, a tremendous sound system and a stage set which included six Roman columns erected across the back of that stage. The band also incorporates video into their stage performance. A huge screen perched high above the audience alternates images of the band on stage with scenes from Duran videos and other interesting footage. The average Duran show is about an hour and a half long and comes replete with the group's many hit singles like "Rio," "Hungry Like the Wolf," "Is There Something I Should Know," and more recent smash hits like "Union of the Snake" and "The Reflex."

The Duran Duran image has been both a blessing and a curse. The critics and the media have chosen to exploit and categorize the band (as critics almost always seem to do) and often misrepresent them. The Durans feel that the glamour-boy, sex idol image has been foisted upon them more by the media than by their own behavior. But this doesn't bother the members of the band too much anymore. Duran Duran know that the devoted fans appreciate them for more than what they look like. To the fans, they represent a new genre of positive thinking to the younger generation. They have made their success on their own and they have convinced the world that dreams are attainable through positive thinking and hard work. The core of Duran Duran's success is the sheer pleasure they bring through their infectious night music. In time, more and more people will stop looking and criticizing and pigeonholing this act, and just listen to that fabulous music.

3. Humble Beginnings

If there is one person responsible for Duran Duran's existence (for the sake of argument, we will exclude their parents, without whom there would of course be no Andy, John, Nick, Roger or Simon at all), it has to be bassist John Taylor. John, the founding father of the group, and his younger friend Nick Rhodes (then Nick Bates) lived right around the corner from each other in a suburb of the industrial city of Birmingham, England. Together they shared an avid interest in music. In fact, they were the only kids in their neighborhood hip enough to own copies of

David Bowie's *The Rise and Fall of Ziggy Stardust* album. Besides their interest in music, they shared an interest in wanting to do something spectacular with their lives. "I have an immense ambition," says Nick today, "and I have always had a very vivid impression of what I wanted to do." From the very start, Nick wanted to be a rock star.

For a sixteen-year-old boy Nick had some very sophisticated ideas about music. Although he had very little formal musical background, he was an avid listener all of his life. Nick was inspired by Roxy Music, one of the first "art rock" bands of the seventies. An art rock band, like Roxy and Yes, was one that combined rock & roll with lush orchestrations to create an almost classical sound. Synthesizers were a big part of the art-rock sound. Nick was in awe of the wistful and elegant keyboard work of Roxy's Bryan Ferry. Even at that very young age, Nick had some very solid ideas about the kind of music he wanted to make.

Back in 1978, John Taylor was eighteen years old. Fresh out of high school, he had some idea of attending art school. That ambition was left by the wayside when he started to spend a lot of time at a very fashionable club called the Barbarella Club. Inspired by the club scene, he and sixteen-year-old Nick decided to start a band—though neither played any instruments.

No matter—they bought a couple of used instruments (Nick a synth box and John a guitar) and recruited some local musicians (Simon Colley on clarinet and bass and Steve Duffey on vocals). They called themselves Duran Duran and, presto—they were a band.

In 1978 England was in the midst of the punk rage, an era of music created by the youth of Britain who were fed up and disgusted with the rock establishment that existed in the seventies. So they invented punk music, designed to express anger and revulsion. The music was abrasive and raw, with very basic rhythms and aggressive lyrics. The musicians of the punk era were untrained for the most part and made fashion statements with their severely cropped hair, black leather and sado-masochistic bondage gear. Bands like the Clash and the Jam were inspiring what John Taylor called "sort of tribal movements, a gang mentality." It was a very political movement aimed to congregate the masses and get them all to do the same thing.

Between 1978 and 1980, John and Nick worked on creating a specific sound for this band they had formed. As they came to master their instruments, they began to discuss the idea of combining rock and disco. It was this slick combination, so refreshing after the harsh punk era, that gave Duran Duran its unique sound. With their less radical and more romantic look and sound, Duran Duran began to make some waves as part of the new music movement. Small waves, but waves nonetheless. By 1980 the band had attracted a fairly significant following in and around Birmingham.

The band suffered some heavy personnel turnovers in those two years. Nick would later refer to this time as "the hellish years with dozens of musicians passing through." Colley and Duffey abruptly departed with a need to pursue more straightforward rock & roll endeavors. Nick and John were back to square one—an ambitious duo in search of the right people to make them a real band. They recruited a new vocalist, Andy Wickett, to fill the gap left by Duffey. They began auditioning drummers to complete their sound. Roger Taylor, then twenty years old and no relation to John, came fresh from a band called the Scent Organs. He auditioned and was selected to join the Duran Duran lineup. Together the new quartet recorded a demo tape which included the first version of what would later become a major hit: "Girls on Film." But just as things began to look good, another personnel change put the group back. For unknown reasons, Andy Wickett quit the group. He was soon replaced by yet a third vocalist: Jeff Thomas. Meanwhile, inspired by Roger's drumming and influenced by several new American rhythm &

blues groups, particularly Chic (at the time the premier black disco group in New York), John Taylor decided to swap his guitar for a bass. Now, a new guitarist was needed. The remaining members decided to place a music press ad and perhaps find the perfect man for the job this time. "Modern guitarist for Roxy/Bowie influenced band" read the ad, and along came John Curtis, a Londoner. But within a few weeks he too decided to hit the road—and he took vocalist Thomas with him.

Who can blame Nick Rhodes for feeling frustrated? He was determined to get things moving at a faster pace. After all, he was already eighteen years old and he wanted to be a rock star. Dreams of being a real band seemed impossibly far away. Musicians were coming and going faster than Nick and John could keep track of them. The sound the duo were hoping to achieve was just not happening. But John and Nick were persistent. They had drive, and despite the hard times they continued to work at their creation. They realized, however, that they needed help. In a slick, businesslike move, Nick decided to pay a visit to the swankiest disco in Birmingham, The Rum Runner Club. The owners of the Rum Runner were two brothers, Paul and Michael Berrow. As Nick remembers: "The Rum Runner was full of businessmen with trendy shirts on, but it was also the hippest club in town." As it turned out, the Berrow brothers were as eager to make their mark on the British club scene and the rock world as the struggling members of Duran Duran were. The brothers had just returned from a trip to New York where they had discovered the famous Studio 54. It became their dream to turn the Rum Runner into a similar club for the young, the trendy and the fashionable. Enter Duran Duran. It didn't take long for the Berrows to see that this slick trio with the rhythmic style of modern dance music and the all-new pretty boy look was just what the doctor ordered. After listening to the band's demo tape, the Berrows agreed not only to let the band play at the Rum Runner but also to manage them and provide rehearsal space in the club.

As managers and mentors, the Berrows took a careful hand in shaping the group's lineup and, more importantly, their image. They felt it was necessary to present Duran Duran as a complete package, different from other pop-rock groups. This made perfect sense to both Nick and John. As Nick recalls: "I think the image was very important for us, after the music. Let's face it, everybody who's been massive in the past twenty years has had a bloody strong image." And the strong-willed, ambitious Mr. Rhodes wanted Duran Duran to be massive. But before they could complete the image, they had to complete the membership. That meant finding a guitarist and a vocalist that would perfectly complement the trio of Taylor, Taylor and Rhodes.

The Berrows concluded that to choose two musicians from the local pool of available players was not the answer. They decided to place an ad in the British music paper, *Melody Maker*, for a "live wire guitarist." Many capable musicians responded, but none that quite fit the bill. Finally, down from Newcastle, came twenty-one-year-old Andy Taylor (again, no relation). At sixteen, Andy had left home to tour Europe with a band. He had just returned from one of his tours when he saw the ad in *Melody Maker*.

Andy auditioned. He was perfect. Both the Berrows and the Durans felt that Andy had the musical capabilities they were looking for and would be an excellent complement to the sound Duran Duran had been perfecting and honing since 1978. The strong, stylish rock leads and the funky rhythms were all there. In fact, Andy seemed like a dream come true for the Durans and the Berrows—at last a guitarist who had the talent and charisma to round out the Duran sound! But the Duran Duran image was as important as the sound at this point. Would Andy be interested in a poseur band? This was an important ingredient to the Duran Duran formula and a delicate situation. John and Nick and the Berrows decided to be upfront with this potential new guitarist. As Andy remembers: " 'We're poseurs,' they said, 'We want a good looking, poseur band.' " But the handsome Mr. Taylor didn't even bat an eye at their straightforwardness. "Good," he said, "because I love dressing up and wearing makeup!" That was all the Berrows and the Durans needed to hear. They had secured themselves the guitarist of their dreams. All they needed was a suitable vocalist.

Simon Le Bon (yes, that is his real name), then twenty-two, was a drama student at the University of Birmingham when the Berrows invited him down to the Rum Runner to strut his stuff, as they say. His ex-girlfriend was a barmaid at the Rum Runner. When she caught word of the dilemma facing the burgeoning rock & roll band, she was quick to recommend her old friend Simon.

Simon arrived at the Rum Runner for his audition wearing leopard-skin pants, a brown suede jacket, pointed boots and dark glasses. He walked into the rehearsal carrying his book of lyrics and drawings and said, "My name is Le Bon." John Taylor recalls the first meeting: "No, I thought, he can't really be called *Le Bon*!"

Simon's audition nearly knocked the Durans and the Berrows over. His voice was smooth and melodic. He was capable of achieving a low, sexy range as well as a higher, sweeter-sounding vocal. Not only could he sing, but he was an absolute character on stage. He danced and strutted, packing feeling and excitement into his vocal delivery. Of course, it was easy for Simon. He was an actor and he was just playing a role, a character—one, as it turned out, that would make him famous. Simon proved himself to be as ambitious as the rest. Although, he admits, at first he didn't realize just how serious they were about the creation of Duran Duran. He says, "I thought it was just going to be a hobby thing. Then I realized they meant business, real business." Simon left the Rum Runner that night christened the official lead singer for Duran Duran, an honor that he celebrated by writing a song called "The Sound of Thunder." The song eventually appeared on the band's debut album.

The Duran Duran we know today played their first gig together at the Edinburgh Festival in July of 1980. It was such a personal success for Simon that he quit the university drama school once and for all. He knew he had found his career. The quintet began playing locally at the Rum Runner's "Roxy/Bowie

Nights" and also in London clubs throughout the summer and early fall of that year.

The Berrows had a tremendous amount of confidence in this band they had taken under their wing. The Durans had the perfect amount of rock, pop and disco combined in their music to make it big. A band like this is just what the music business was lacking in the early eighties. In order to finance the first Duran Duran tour, Michael Berrow sold his house. He booked the band as the very unlikely opening act for political activist and singer Hazel O'Connor, who had been enjoying her own success with her record and movie *Breaking Glass*. Once on the road and out of Birmingham, Duran Duran began attracting the attention of record companies who were quick to take notice of these five new faces emerging on the rock scene. By autumn of 1980, the band had signed with EMI Records. Their first single was released and . . . well, the rest you know already.

Success didn't exactly come knocking on Duran Duran's door. They went to success and pounded on its gates until it let them in. In short, these five, young, serious lads *made* it happen with a lot of hard work, a determined outlook and an undying ability to dream.

4. The Fab Five

At this point you are probably wondering: Just who are the men that make up this fabulous band? Where do they come from, and what makes them tick? Although their privacy is well guarded, there is a lot that Duran Duran would like their fans to know about them. That they are genuine people, with drives and ambitions and ideas, is an important part of their popularity as well as an important part of their thriving career. Behind their fairy-tale image is a great deal of hard work. Behind their golden-boy mystique are five adult men that have risen to the challenge of stardom.

Well, for those of you who just can't stand the suspense any longer, here are close-ups of the individuals that comprise the Fab Five.

ANDY TAYLOR—Mad Guitarist

Andy Taylor is Duran Duran's guitarist. He is the second-youngest member of the group. He was born on February 16, 1961 in Whitely Bay, a coastal fishing town in the north of England. Andy taught himself to play the guitar when he was only five years old. By the time he was eleven his father bought him his own electric guitar and he began studying jazz with a nearby neighbor, Dave Black. Since music is not generally considered a respectable or lucrative profession (as opposed to, say, medicine or law), Andy was lucky to have a father who encouraged him to pursue his musical talents. He instinctively felt that music might be Andy's calling in life—and how right he turned out to be!

Andy describes his guitar playing as "a hobby gone mad." He spent most of his life enthralled by the twanging and the thumping of the rock & roll sound that rang profoundly throughout England's famous music scene. Even today during the slow moments of Duran

Duran's rehearsal periods, Andy loves to toss off a crazed guitar solo, mimicking the music he was brought up on. He has been known to leave the other members of the band writhing with laughter. The corny guitar hero poses he strikes to accompany his mad playing has sent an entire studio full of engineers, producers and musicians into hysterics. Besides being the recording studio cut-up, Andy is a fine and serious musician with perhaps more professional experience than any of the other members of the band.

Andy left school when he was sixteen to join a band. He did a series of European tours with them—playing everywhere from military installations to some of the seedier European clubs. He came to his audition for Duran Duran straight from one of these tours and was hired immediately. The other members of Duran Duran were not only wowed by his fantastic guitar playing, but they recognized that his gentle good looks—dark hair, bright, inquisitive eyes (which he often prefers to shade behind a pair of mysterious dark glasses), high cheekbones, a sculptured chin and perfect lips—most definitely fit into the Duran Duran image. Although Andy had many fond memories of playing the Euro-strip club scene as a teenager, he was also frustrated that his career was not moving along. The music was just not happening with those other bands. Deep in his heart he wanted to capture a particular musical sound. He wanted to work with a band that would blend together and create a solid group, a group with a purpose and a direction. He had spent many years perfecting his guitar playing. He was very serious about music and his career. He wanted a band that would allow him to grow. And Duran Duran were just that. Not only was Andy Taylor the perfect guitarist for Duran Duran, Duran Duran was the perfect band for Andy Taylor. Here was his opportunity to grow as a musician, to further his career, and to make his father a very proud man.

For those fans who are by this time drooling passionately over Andy, here's a little bad news: He's married. Andy and his wife, Tracy Wilson (she was formerly the band's hairdresser), were married in a very small ceremony in Los Angeles in August, 1982. Despite the efforts to keep it small and quiet, the blissful event still made the front page of the London daily newspapers. The wedding took place midway between Duran Duran's second tour of the United States, making it a hectic event and not allowing much time for a honeymoon. Nevertheless, Andy and Tracy are very happy. They live together in a fifteenth-century cottage in Shropshire, England, on several acres of land. Tracy and Andy love to raise animals (dogs, cats and more). When they are not in their cottage, they are at their loft in London. Andy and Tracy are expecting their first child very soon. It has been a very difficult few months for Andy. Being on the road and away from his wife at such a crucial time has not been easy. According to John, Andy has been suffering from morning sickness as well as experiencing labor pains during the band's recent tour just to make him feel more at home. No doubt Andy will make a wonderful father and is looking forward to parenthood very much.

Besides his home and his loft, Andy owns a restaurant in his hometown called Rio (sound familiar?). Andy's father, now a carpenter, helped rebuild and remodel it when it was first purchased.

Being on the road a lot is difficult. Andy's most effective cure for homesickness is playing good music with the other members of Duran Duran. "That gives us all a big boost," he says. Like all the Durans, Andy is an extremely hard worker. Sometimes the rigors of the road do take their toll, however. When Duran Duran were on their second world tour, Andy suffered a collapse (from exhaustion) after playing a gig in Australia. His idea of the good life? "Sitting there with the dog watching Russell Harty. What more to life can one ask?"

43

ROGER TAYLOR—The Ground that Cannot Be Shaken

"It's part of my personality to keep a low profile," says Duran drummer Roger Taylor. "I've always been like that. At school I was always at the back of the class. I suppose I was shy." As gentle as he may seem, Roger is very much the backbone of the band. As a matter of fact, John Taylor refers to him as "the ground that cannot be shaken." Roger's calm, down-to-earth temperament helps keep the rest of the band's feet on the ground and their instruments in motion.

Born on April 26, 1960 in Shard End, Birmingham (that's England, not Alabama), Roger began banging on pots with knitting needles at the age of ten. His father worked in the automobile industry, which employed at least seventy-five per cent of the town. "It was either that," says Roger, "or escape." Unlike Andy, Roger did not have a father encouraging all that banging and pounding around the house. In an industrial town like Birmingham, it was expected that a young boy finish school and join the auto industry like his father. Just think, if it weren't for Roger's deep ambition and artistic streak, he could be building cars today instead of creating music with Duran Duran!

Roger made the decision to escape in his mid-teens when he joined a series of bands with bizarre names like Crucified Toad and the Scent Organs. "You could either have escaped through music or through football," added Roger, "and I wasn't much good at football."

Roger left the Scent Organs to hook up with Nick Rhodes and John Taylor in 1978. He became the first drummer and third permanent member of the burgeoning group. In terms of the Duran Duran image, like Andy and the others, Roger fit the bill. His low profile and quiet disposition created a perfect balance with the other Durans who are more outgoing and talkative (especially Simon). His man-of-mystery aura completed the band's personality. Anyone can see that Roger's good looks also add to the Duran Duran image. With his soft brown hair and sensitive dark eyes, he had no trouble being a poseur. His only problem is that he's a little camera-shy. All those flashing cameras and the mobs of groping fans make him a little nervous.

It makes perfect sense that Roger is the so-called backbone of Duran Duran, as music is very much the backbone of Roger's life. He hauls a large selection of records and tapes with him wherever he goes. His playing is influenced by what he hears and his playing in turn is a great source of inspiration to the other Durans, especially when it comes to songwriting. He's an integral part of the Duran Duran creative process that forms their unique chemistry.

Like his fellow Durans, Roger doesn't believe in rock & roll politics. "I don't think bands can change politics," he says. "Look at the Clash, they have been talking about politics for years and they haven't changed anything."

Roger admits that he does not have very many hobbies. To him hobbies are something you do when you get bored and Roger doesn't get bored very often. Music keeps him alive and inspired. For a good time Roger likes to lie in bed and watch television—not a bad way to wind down from the rigors of the road and being chased by girls! But it is difficult for Roger being on the road, away from family and friends and especially his girlfriend. What cheers him up? Playing a great show with the band or laying down some exciting new tracks in the studio. As Roger tells us: "That puts me on top of the world."

SIMON Le BON—Choirboy

Simon Charles Le Bon (the other guys in the band and his close friends call him Charly) was born on October 27, 1958 in Watford Herts just outside of London. At twenty-six he is the oldest member of the band. He grew up in what he calls a totally middle-class household. His mother Ann is now a music teacher in Florida. His father John does something hush-hush for the government. No one will reveal just what that hush-hush job is.

Simon started singing when he was very young; his voice was high and clear then. He joined a church choir and his mother would record him singing all these church songs. "When she plays them for me now," Simon confesses, "it makes me cringe to hear myself."

Simon went to the same high school as Elton John. Later, he attended the University of Birmingham where he studied drama. Simon always had a great affinity for show biz and also a great talent for it. His dream of being on the stage came true when he nailed the ultimate role of lead singer for Duran Duran. Not only did he get to be a famous pop star, but he realized his lifelong dream to act. After all, starring in all those sizzling videos required all the acting skills Simon picked up in drama school, didn't it?

Simon admits he went through the typical rebellious teenager routine with his parents by experimenting with drinking and drugs. But all that passed when he noticed many of his companions turning into speed freaks and drunks by the age of sixteen. When he was seventeen he went through his punk-rock stage which was all the rage throughout England at the time. Simon recalls many nights sleeping on benches in Hyde Park because he either couldn't afford a taxi or missed the last train home. But before long Simon began to develop some ideas about his future. "I decided when I was young that I wanted lots of attention," he says, "and being a show-off got me involved in drama school and the pop group business and that then got me nice girlfriends, so I thought I'd stick at it."

Despite the fact that his handsome face is often smeared across newspapers, magazines, album covers and the like, Simon says he is one hundred percent normal. As he puts it: "People think it takes someone special or different to be a pop star, but it doesn't. I'm absolutely normal. It feels like a big bluff sometimes." Certainly his fans would think otherwise. Simon is very special and very different.

There is no quibbling when it comes to Simon's good looks, and this tall (six-foot-one) handsome singer thinks that good looks are definitely the key to Duran Duran's huge popularity. "That's a big part of it," he says, "though when I first joined the band we all looked like a bunch of weirdos." He continues, "You gradually find out what makes you look good." Initially, Duran Duran became caught up in the "New Romantic" look. Duran Duran has always been a very fashion-conscious band and the frills and ruffles were very in for a while. The look now is much more sophisticated. "I've come a long way from punk," Simon recalls. "Now I wear a pair of jeans one day and an Anthony Price suit the next!" Nevertheless Simon works hard at keeping his image intact and his appearance up to his sophisticated standards. At one point Simon had a bit of a weight problem. Incredibly, the other members of the band used to refer to him as "lardo." Simon now manages to keep his body in shape—as the millions of fans who watch his video shenanigans can testify. Simon feels that knowing how to make yourself look good has a lot to do with how you will appeal to women—and Simon knows a lot about appealing to women.

Simon Le Bon has always had a fascination with women. "I have always been intrigued by girls," he admits. "They have always been an endless source of mystery to me." John Taylor is convinced that Simon often writes in a specific way so that the band can work with beautiful and interesting women while shooting videos. But Simon's philosophy concerning women is a sound one. "It's not really so much what you make yourself look like, but it's an attitude you have toward women in your mind.

If you're frightened of women, I don't think you're ever going to appeal to them." Simon always had dreams of finding the perfect girl and he doesn't think there is anything old-fashioned about wanting to settle down.

When Simon isn't at work or on the road with Duran Duran, he stays at home with his girlfriend Claire Stansfield in their apartment in Toronto (they're still looking for a place in London). It seems Simon has found that girl he's always wanted in Claire. The couple are engaged to be married. When Simon and Claire first began seeing each other, the press simply went crazy. Everyone wanted to know who she was. For a while Simon was adamant about keeping his love life a secret. Eventually, as the couple began to make more public appearances together, the lovely lady's identity was revealed.

In his spare time Simon writes, draws and reads anything from science fiction to Shakespeare. Simon enjoys the finer things in life and this is probably the happiest he has ever been in his life. What are some of his favorite things? Good films (anything by Fellini), good wine (a dry white) and being on stage with lots of girls screaming their heads off. That really cheers him up.

NICK RHODES — Rock Entrepreneur

He was born Nicholas James Bates on June 8, 1962 in Hollywood, Birmingham (just down the road from John Taylor). The keyboard player, Nick is the youngest member of Duran Duran. Nick's mother Sylvia has always been a happy housewife and his father, Roger, an engineer. Nick and John knew each other as children, and grew up together sharing an avid interest in music. They were the first kids in their neighborhood to take an interest in emerging talents like David Bowie and Roxy Music, which was a very hip thing for two young boys from the suburbs.

Nick was not very interested in school. He left because he felt that he could do better trying to start a band. He says: "I didn't really feel that I needed to know what sodium bicarbonate and sulphuric acid makes." With a jaunty and bubbly personality, Nick was not the sort of teenager who was content just to daydream. Even at the tender age of sixteen, Nick had an intense ambition and a lot of determination. He always knew what he wanted to do and he wasn't going to let anyone or anything stand in his way.

From the start, Nick wanted to make rock & roll music. He fiddled around with keyboards

CYNTHIA C. KENT

dreaming of being a rock star. When he was sixteen, he quit school to start a band with his good friend John. Nick invested the small amount of money he had saved in his first synth box—Duran Duran at its most humble beginnings. In true rock star fashion, Nick changed his name from Bates to Rhodes. "Simply for aesthetic reasons," he says today.

As keyboard player, Nick enjoys working in the studio more than the others. It gives him a chance to really work at the music he puts down on tape and trace the progression of his style. Always a perfectionist, Nick will do his part over and over again until he feels it's the absolute best it can be. As much satisfaction as he derives from studio work, Nick confides "there's nothing quite like putting on a live show and being the object of all that fan adoration."

Aside from Duran Duran, Nick has completed several independent projects. Last year he produced Kajagoogoo's smash debut album and their hit single, "Too Shy." Nick met Kajagoogoo's ex-lead singer, Limahl one steamy night in a small London club. As he recalls the meeting: "I was minding my business having a quiet drink when this two-tones, spiky haired chap came along. I liked what he was saying and it reminded me of Duran Duran before we recorded 'Planet Earth.' " The two musicians quickly sealed a pact to work together when time permitted. Nick helped the band get a contract with EMI Records (the mother company to the Duran's Capitol in America). They finally got together in the studio several months later. "Too Shy" was a smash and the rest is history.

Nick is also an avid photographer. Photography has always been a hobby, but recently Nick has been at work on a book of experimental photos called *Abstract Polaroids*. He plans to have an exhibition upon the book's release. By the same token, Nick has an ardent interest in video and film. He says he has always been interested in film ever since he was a kid and would someday ("in future years—a long time off," he says) like to direct films.

Nick is engaged to a beautiful girl named Juliana Friedman. The happy couple plan to tie the knot in the near future. Like Simon, Nick has always yearned to settle down with the girl of his dreams and is very happy that he's found her at last.

Like Andy, Nick has invested a lot of his Duran Duran money in a new home. His new house is in London, but at present, Nick says, "It's a total wreck." He has plans to completely refurbish the house and then redecorate in all art deco (one other passion) and is very excited about the prospect.

Nick is the band's jokester; he is always good for breaking up a tense moment in the studio with a good laugh. Like Simon he takes pride in his good looks and probably enjoys wearing makeup more than the other guys. He loves all animals and hates it when narrow-minded people bring innocent animals to any harm. One of his favorite companions is his cat Sebastian. Other passions: He loves a good steak and strawberries, though not together. Last but not least, Nick likes to smile. Yes, Nick smiles a lot. And why not? He's got a lot to smile about.

JOHN TAYLOR—"P. R." Man

John Taylor, ex-guitarist and now bass player, is the founding father of Duran Duran and most often spokesperson for the group. He was born Nigel John Taylor in Hollywood, a suburb of Birmingham, on June 20, 1960. His first name embarrasses him; he prefers to be called John. Actually, no one except his parents call him Nigel. John's father is a white collar worker in the auto industry just like Roger's, and his mother works in a school cafeteria. It was John and good friend Nick that started the wheels turning of what would ultimately become the supergroup of the eighties.

John got his first guitar when he was only fifteen. He played for four years, enjoying the sound, growing with the instrument. But when he heard the funky bass grooves of a band called Chic, he discovered that putting down the bass lines was really his calling in life.

John is Duran Duran's nighttime P.R. man. That is, he likes to party and can often persuade other members of the band to party along with him. He describes himself as "a pretty cheerful sort of chap. One who likes going out to parties and clubs, seeing and being seen." John admits that, like Simon, he is also "girl crazy." He and Simon most enjoy the crowds of dazzling women which loyally follow the band around when they are on tour. Although he does have a steady girlfriend, he still likes having lots of girls around.

John Taylor just might be the favorite among Duran Duran fans. With his sultry good looks and outgoing personality, fans can't help losing their hearts to him. And John is quite a charmer. He has a certain magnetism that makes him stand out in a crowd and his intelligence and wit have made him a favorite with journalists. He has a great deal of enthusiasm that shows in everything he does.

John is an open and likable sort of guy. To the extent that any one person is the leader of

Duran Duran, John is it. He is most often the one to offer an opinion to the press during an interview—there is no doubt that John has a lot to say. Unfortunately the way the band is treated by the press is often infuriating and John feels driven to the screaming point. "We're not the shallow pop group the critics think we are," he says. "I think if they knew us as people, and knew that we're genuine and weren't put together by a record company, then they might not be so critical."

John possesses a wild fascination for fast and sporty cars. He recently bought a gold Aston Martin and he has his eye on a fancy gull-winged Mercedes. His automotive dream is to own a different car for every day of the week.

John is the only member of the band that still lives in his home town of Birmingham. He bought the house some time ago, but hasn't spent much time there at all. In fact, in a recent interview he stated that he had only been there once. Sometimes life on the road "is like a nightmare," says John. No wonder he needs all those parties to cheer him up. John bought a flat in London before touring America for the third time.

John's other passion? James Bond flicks. For relaxation he curls up and pops a James Bond video into his video recorder. He digs

Bond, he admits, "to the point of obsession." That explains the gold Aston Martin—a famous James Bond car from the movie *Goldfinger,* one of John's all-time favorite Bond flicks. He owns a complete set of Bond films on video. Just as Roger hauls his records and tapes everywhere, John always carries his videos with him on the road. In fact, John's current flame is actress and model Janine Andrews, who appeared in the recent Bond film *Octopussy.*

Much like the other Durans, though, John's favorite activity is making music. Being on stage is what it's all about. A last fantasy: John has always wanted to go out with a Charlie's Angel.

There they are, one by one, the members of Duran Duran. John, Nick, Andy, Roger and Simon are a very authentic group of young individuals with unique talents. And all are obsessed by the same thing—making fabulous music.

5. What's a Duran?

What's in a name? For a rock & roll band — a lot. And naming a band is not an easy task by any means. After all, what you call yourself should be easy to remember, and should roll off the tongue to make it easy for the DJs, journalists, publicists and other people who will influence your success. No band or recording artist wants to fall into that problematic scenario where a song becomes a hit and all anyone can say about them is, "Oh, you know, the ones who do that song . . ." Therefore, calling your band the Antidisestablishmentarianism Band is most definitely not a good idea.

Usually a band is named after one of its members, like Van Halen (easy enough) or the Alan Parsons Project. Others choose something simple or easy to remember, like Yes. Or even a place, like Berlin or Alabama. Then again, some have chosen a name that best describes the group, like Motley Crue. Which leaves us to ponder just where the Psychedelic Furs got their name.

So where did the name Duran Duran come from? It only takes a quick scan to see that no one in the band is actually named Duran. Members are Simon Le Bon, John Taylor, Andy Taylor, Roger Taylor and Nick Rhodes—plenty of Taylors but no Durans. And I can't think of any place in the world called Duran. Can you? So, what is it then? Well, it's all actually very simple.

Influenced by the chic Barbarella club in England, and being a great fan of the classic 1960s science fiction film *Barbarella* starring Jane Fonda, John Taylor decided to draw on that inspiration. Actually calling themselves Barbarella might have caused confusion, since that was the name of the fancy club. And it might have been a little bit pretentious. Besides, Barbarella is just not that much fun to say. Then they wanted to call themselves RAF—but let's face it, that's just not too catchy. Durand Durand was the name of another character—the villain—in *Barbarella*. The role was played by Milo O'Shea. If you drop the d's you get Duran Duran. Now there's an interesting name. It was agreed upon unanimously. Duran Duran it was.

For those of you who have never seen the movie—you should. But until you can catch it rerunning on late night TV or on a Sunday afternoon, here's a little bit about the flick to give you the full flavor of the wittiness of Duran Duran's name.

The setting is the year 40,000. At the opening of the film, our heroine, Barbarella (played superbly by Jane Fonda in her pre-political activist and workout days) is racing through space in her very sexy Alpha 7 spacecraft toward the planet Capri for a long-awaited and well-deserved vacation. Barbarella is a champion astronaut—sort of an outer space James Bond (maybe that's what attracted John to the film in the first place). Her job: to vanquish evil wherever she finds it.

The Alpha 7, by the way, is not your average spacecraft. In no way does it resemble the cold, metallic confines of a current Apollo spacecraft or space shuttle. The Alpha 7 is a multi-hued, odd-shaped ship with a hedonistic design. The film's production notes called it a "cross between a sexy lawnmower and a chest X-ray of

Mae West." From each side bulge three "breathing" lungs which heave in and out during flight. Inside, the floors and walls are covered with a deep pile gold fur. With the flick of a hidden switch, the paintings by Renoir and the Op Art which cover the walls slide back and reveal all the control devices.

Before she has a chance to land and pursue her vacation, Barbarella's course is interrupted by an urgent call from Earth's president. He orders Barbarella on a special mission—to find Durand Durand. Durand Durand is an earth scientist who has been missing for several years. He carries with him the secret of the Positronic Ray, a most evil and ultimate weapon. As our heroine begins her mission, her spacecraft is thrown out of control by a magnetic storm, and she is forced to crash land on a strange and mysterious planet called Lythion.

While Barbarella is examining the ship for damage, she is approached by the two lovely blond twins, Stomaxys and Glassina. The two ladies are not so lovely in temperament. They attack Barbarella and tie her up. The twins bring Barbarella to the wreckage of a spaceship marked Alph 1. Here the twins keep their collection of dolls. Not your ordinary dolls, mind you, but vicious little dolls whose smiling mouths contain rows of sharklike teeth. The savage little dolls attack Barbarella. But before they have a chance to devour her alive, she is rescued by Mark Hand, a handsome, bearded astronaut played by Ugo Tognazzi. As a gesture of her thanks, Barbarella makes love to the handsome saviour and then bids him goodbye. It's back to the Alpha 7 and on with her important mission.

Barbarella takes off for the planet Sogo, once again in search of Durand Durand. Landing again, she comes up against another problem. Her spacecraft plunges thousands of feet into the ground and she finds herself in a complicated labyrinth deep beneath Sogo's surface. Here she meets the blind angel, Pygar with his majestic snow-white wings. Pygar introduces her to professor Ping, played by Marcel Marceau, an orchid-chewing old man who has been banished along with Pygar to the maze beneath the terrible and baroque city of Sogo. Ping urges Barbarella to the planet's surface where he is sure she will find Durand Durand. Pygar agrees to fly her there with his wings. Before they can get underway, they are attacked by one of the Tyrant's Black Guards. Pygar crushes the guard and saves Barbarella. She thanks him in the same way she thanked her first rescuer. With the aid of Barbarella's mercury-gyro wrist compass and Pygar's wings, once again they are off for Sogo.

When they finally arrive in the city, on a

dark street they find a door marked "The Ultimate Solution." Upon entering they discover the floor is made up of a moving, transparent liquid called Mathmos. It is the living lake upon which Sogo is built. Suddenly, they are surrounded by more of the infamous Black Guards. The Black Guards bring the two before the Concierge. Pygar is taken away in a net and Barbarella is brought before the Great Tyrant, the Black Queen. After a confrontation, the Black Guard throws open a set of doors and reveals to Barbarella, Pygar, his great wings crucified against a wall.

Barbarella is then thrown into a cage with hundreds of birds that attack her. Before they can kill her, a trap door flys open and our heroine plunges down a long, dark chute into the arms of Dildano (played by David Hemmings). Dildano, she discovers, is the leader of a revolutionary group that is out to usurp the Black Queen. Barbarella agrees to aid Dildano in return for his help in finding Durand Durand. However, when she returns to the palace, the Concierge captures her again and tries to torture her with his Excessive Machine. Her sentence is "death from pleasure." But a champion astronaut like Barbarella proves to be too much even for the machine, which blows a fuse and goes up in a gigantic puff of smoke.

The Concierge becomes furious (he spent a

long time on that machine). It is at this time that Barbarella recognizes the Concierge as her long-sought quarry—the villainous Durand Durand! By now, Durand Durand is a raving maniac. He shows Barbarella his secret Positronic Ray, which is capable of transforming living matter into a state of ever-melting, perpetual agony—surely, the ultimate weapon. He also confesses his plot to kill the Black Queen and become ruler of Sogo. "Nothing can stop me now," he raves. "Today Sogo, tomorrow the Earth, then master of the universe!"

Re-enter Dildano and the revolutionaries. They shatter Durand Durand's dream of evil. A mad and defeated Durand runs to the palace tower where he aims his Positronic Ray in a great arc over Sogo, killing the revolutionaries, Professor Ping and Dildano. The Black Queen, in despair, pulls a hidden switch, freeing the slimy Mathmos which hungrily gobbles up Durand Durand and all of Sogo. Since the Mathmos lives only off of evil, Barbarella is spared. In her innocence, she is indigestible. As the terrible city of Sogo crumbles around her, a freed Pygar whisks her up into his strong arms. Together, they return to safety.

Barbarella recaptured the spirit of American comic strips of the early days, that was fast vanishing in the late sixties. It recaptured the essence of fantasy—when even the impossible was impossible. The movie has become a sci-fi classic and somewhat of a cult film since its release. Based on the adult illustrated feature book created by Jean Claude Forest, the film is marked by the same mixture of fantasy and humor and beauty and horror. Not only is it an adventure, but also a biting, often humorous allegorical commentary on sex, politics, and society.

6. The Band Made in Videoland

Although music video seems to have sprung up quite suddenly in the past two years, it's a medium that was tapped by rock & roll artists many years before. Devo, for instance, is a group whose innovative sound has been linked to fascinating images since the 1970s. Their album-length videos, *The Men Who Make the Music* (1979), and the more recent, *We're All Devo* (1983), were fine examples of the magic that can be made by wedding sound with image. Devo has certainly been a great video influence on any rock bands of the 1980s. A great deal of concert footage from bands of the

sixties and seventies are available on video to-
day. Artists like the Beatles, Cream, Deep
Purple, Emerson, Lake and Palmer, and the
Doors have all been immortalized on video.

As many of you well know, several feature
films have been based on spectacular rock &
roll events. *Woodstock, Celebration at Big Sur*
and *The Last Waltz* are just a few examples of
films that have superbly captured the spirit of
rock & roll music and portrayed rock artists of
the sixties and seventies as positive and creative
forces.

But the idea of using video as a promotional
tool is a new idea and one that has developed
furiously in the last two years. And the amount
of money being spent to create the videos that
we see every day on MTV is forever increasing.
A simple performance video may or may not
cost a lot, depending on what the artist has in
mind. Van Halen's recent "Jump" video was ru-
mored to have cost only six hundred dollars,
whereas other artists have chosen to produce
full-blown conceptualized videos like Michael
Jackson's "Thriller," which cost a record breaking one-and-a-half million dollars.

1983 was perhaps *the* year of the video music
revolution. More bands in all genres of
music—pop, rock, disco, adult contemporary,
soul, jazz and country—made videos than ever
before. As the demand for video became larger,

more video music programs began to appear. Besides MTV, other cable stations introduced their own video programs like *NightTracks* and the networks began to get in on the act with shows like *Friday Night Videos* and *Top 40 Videos*. With programming expanding at this rate, the quality and creativity involved in making a video expanded enormously. Established film makers suddenly took an interest in the new form. Top commercial directors like Bob Giraldi (Michael Jackson) began testing the waters as well as noted film directors like Bob Rafelson (Lionel Richie's "All Night Long") and John Landis ("Thriller"). Dance was rediscovered as a natural video medium while computer graphics and animation began to emerge as inventive alternatives to the usual video fare. Not only were the major record-selling artists making videos, but so were the lesser-known and up-and-coming performers. It suddenly was more important to make a video than it was to record a demo tape. MTV introduced "The Basement Tapes," which gave airtime to young bands trying to score a record contract and attract the public's attention.

There is no doubt that the age of video music is upon us. Practically every rock performer can testify that video shows are becoming a greater and greater force in the industry, and all will agree that it's a heaven-sent promotional tool for the new artist. The bottom line is that a recording artist today must be visual to even keep a foothold in the market. A little bit of exposure goes a long long way!

Duran Duran has been labeled "the band made in video land." "If it weren't for MTV," says lead singer Simon Le Bon, "we'd still be the same unknown group from England with the funny name." When the group's video of the single "Hungry Like the Wolf" aired on the twenty-four hour music channel in 1982, viewers—especially the female ones—hungered with a wolflike appetite for more of the five, devil-may-care, gorgeous boys they had witnessed tumbling through the jungles of Sri Lanka in search of the elusive black beauty in war paint. The video clip, directed by the award-winning Russell Mulcahy (of 10cc fame), was perhaps the single most important element in propelling the band to the ranks of American superstardom. Due to the enormous fan response, the video went into immediate heavy rotation on the cable channel and could be seen up to four times a day by the fast-rising cult of Duranies.

"When we first did the video," said John Taylor, "it was just another promotional tool. But all of a sudden we had a hit single in Australia. Then the same thing happened in the States, all because they were showing this bloody video. Pop music," he went on to add, "has now become three dimensional."

Certainly, many other talented bands were making interesting videos at the time. But not very many were achieving the same overnight success as the Fab Five. Why? Well, the band's good looks had a lot to do with it. But other artists look good. Look at Sting of the Police or Rick Springfield. It was also the overall positiveness of the clip which took the audience by the horns—the idea of fighting for something and fighting seemingly impossible obstacles to win it. The video's underlying message was "never give up." The music is catchy and bouncy, the lyrics are sexy and seductive, the locale was equally seductive and *new*. The setting was *Casablanca*-esque, giving the impression that this was just a trailer for a full-length motion picture rather than just a three-minute music video.

Personally, I remember the first time I heard "Hungry Like the Wolf" on MTV. I tuned into MTV while staying at a friend's house that summer. As I puttered around the house doing other things, I suddenly heard this song coming from the TV. I raced in to see what it was—it sounded so great. I caught the end of what looked like a terrific video. A few weeks later, while at the office, "Hungry Like the Wolf" came on the radio. I turned to a friend and

71

asked who the group was. She told me it was Duran Duran. I was hooked!

What sets Duran Duran apart from other rock groups as video stars is a unique blend of musical and visual drive—they conceive their music not only as sound, but also as image. With their virtually unmatched ease in front of a rolling camera, the members of Duran Duran are able to translate their songs and lyrics into beautiful and uncanny images. The "Hungry Like the Wolf" video was fun and exciting. Duran Duran was one of the first bands to stage something fun in an exotic locale. The cable-viewing audience was tired of watching people standing on a stage singing and the Duran Duran video was a breath of fresh air.

It's no wonder then, that Duran Duran were among the first to package their first eleven videos onto one hour-long video cassette. Released by Thorn/EMI, the Duran Duran video LP has so far been the undisputed video champ. It was recently awarded a gold award by the Record Industry Association of America (RIAA) for selling over one million copies. Each of the videos included on the tape are from the *Duran Duran* or the *Rio* LPs and are considered to be small video masterpieces—paragons of the art of video making. It's worth taking a look at what you can see on this tape. For those of you who already own it, maybe you should watch it again today, and for those of you who don't, maybe this will make you think about buying one.

The Duran Duran Video LP

"RIO"

Filmed on the beautiful, tropical island of Antigua, "Rio" was the second video to make a splash with regular MTV viewers. The band is seen aboard a luxurious yacht singing the praises of a girl named Rio (named after the Rio Grande, the river that separates Mexico and Texas). According to the song, she's a perfect ten. "Rio" is full of offbeat seashore humor. Drummer Roger Taylor suavely approaches a lovely bathing beauty only to have his advances curtailed by a sand crab suddenly (and painfully) attaching itself to his foot. He falls awkwardly into the water and the pretty lady laughs. The camera cuts to an innocent-looking John Taylor curled up reading a comic book. Simon picks up a telephone on board the yacht to speak to the adored Rio who floats by on a nearby raft. A brief tug on the phone wire and she sends a rakish Simon overboard. The very observant will notice that Simon is wearing flippers: the perfect complement to his white suit. Pink and yellow liquid is poured into elegant champagne glasses and served up to one of the Durans who is appropriately clad in an air tank and goggles. He plunges down and drinks the liquid under water, filling the surrounding blue water with pink and yellow swirls. Rio tosses a small ball that grows and grows until it becomes a *giant* beach ball that chases a bikini-clad Simon off the pier into the ocean. He is pulled ashore by the bathing beauty in a fisherman's net. Quite a catch.

One of the highlights of the clip is the thrilling saxophone solo performed by Nick aboard a floating raft and John on a grass-covered hilltop. Other highlights: Simon gallops a chestnut horse down an empty beach; John and Andy parody their own musicianship with make-believe saxophones and a fully clothed Andy Taylor gets thrown overboard by the other band members in what looks like a blooper they decided to use.

All in all, everyone has a great time running around on the sunny beach. This is definitely a funny and happy video — a must-see for every Duran Duran fan.

"PLANET EARTH"

A far cry from the seaside shenanigans on the beaches of Antigua, "Planet Earth" brings us back to the early days of Duran Duran. It was the band's first hit single from the debut *Duran Duran* LP. The clip, also directed by Russell Mulcahy, begins with a blue-toned special-effects shot of Roger, his head perched in slow-moving clouds in front of a huge earth. He tosses his head back in slow motion as the camera cuts to the band performing on a futuristic set — something resembling a huge iceberg planted in a room made of dizzying glass. Simon dances on a propless white set while boxes of color descend and freeze him in time. Then we see him engulfed in flames. He sings the song's chorus: "Look now, look all around, there's no sign of life," before succumbing to the fire. The action cuts to a black-and-white scene and a reclining, bare-chested Simon sings to the camera. The song contains some ironic lyrics: "Some new romantic looking for a TV sound, you'll see I'm right some other time" — a strange foreshadowing of the group's future.

From the performance sequence, the clip cuts to some close, shadowy shots of band members singing the song's refrain ("This is planet earth, planet earth, planet earth") while beneath them a computer printout of population statistics roll by. Other highlights: some good close shots of Roger behind the drums; two strange-looking, barefoot, punk dancers watched by a curious John. The clip ends with a freeze frame of Simon leaping off the iceberg into the deep and dark abyss below.

"LONELY IN YOUR NIGHTMARE"

"Lonely in Your Nightmare" is a very tender, moving sensual clip. Simon, clad in a leather jacket, enters a dusty, abandoned building and finds a photograph on the floor. The photo is the freeze frame of Simon jumping into the darkness from the preceding "Planet Earth" video. He dusts off the cryptic photo and climbs a staircase. Once upstairs, he goes to a large window and looks out over a black-and-white London. He gazes pensively at a woman in black on the street. He sings: "Even on the darkest night when empty promise means empty hand." The clip becomes color as Simon finds the same woman sleeping. She writhes slowly in dream over the wrinkled sheets as Simon leans close to her ear and sings: "Because you're lonely in your nightmare, let me in."

From the stark black-and-white shots of a dreary London, the video cuts to a colorful Sri Lanka where a dreamy Simon walks along an empty beach. The mysterious lady beckons him from across the water. He walks toward her. They meet, they embrace, they dance. Is he dreaming? Is she? No one knows for sure.

Other members of the band are seen searching for the same mysterious woman on crowded streets. John sees her from across a park bench for a fleeting moment before she vanishes again. The scene returns to the window overlooking London where individual band members turn thoughtfully from the window to gaze pensively into the camera in a lingering shot. Simon sings once again for the sleeping lady to "let him in," but she remains asleep.

"CARELESS MEMORIES"

"Careless Memories" was the follow-up single to "Planet Earth." Both singles come from the *Duran Duran* LP. Directed by Perry Haines, it is one of the few clips not directed by Russell Mulcahy. The video opens with the band riding in the back seat of a car. An enviable young girl is wedged between Nick and John who are more concerned with the scenery passing by. As the clip continues we come to understand that this woman is the object of Simon's "careless memories." Intercut with scenes of the band in performance are shots of a modern, starkly white room (except for a painting on the wall and a vase full of colorful tulips) where Nick, John, Roger and Andy hang out in the background while in the foreground

Simon sings of love lost. In a climatic moment Simon reaches for the tulips (which seem to be a symbol of the lady lost) and hurls them angrily into the air. We watch as they fly up in slow motion. As they slowly cascade to the ground the camera freezes them in silent motion. Love letters torn into pieces are blown off the glass-and-chrome coffee table. The video ends with an explosive moment as Simon flings open the door of the darkened room and a blast of white light shoots in from behind him. Forming his hand into the shape of a pistol, he shoots at the love letters flying around the room while he sings: "Look out! Look out! Look out!" He drops to one knee, turns profile, and blows the invisible smoke from the barrel of his imaginary gun. Freeze frame.

"MY OWN WAY"

"My Own Way" is a snappy, dance-oriented piece released between the *Duran Duran* and *Rio* LPs. The lyrics reflect the band's move toward independence from London's Blitz movement. Gone are the frilly shirts; the band is into leather and tuxedos here. This is a performance video in a studio setting. The dominant colors are black and red — very Latin. A bullfighter swirls his red satin cape while Spanish women in high heels dance around the band. The video is characterized by split screens and the cutting of the screen into many geometric patterns. A parrot that dances on Nick's keyboards steals the show. The Spanish dancers release a virtual galaxy of brightly colored, glittering confetti from the folds of their skirts which cascade all about the stage. Nick and Roger change into formal tuxedos and someone runs a single red rose sensuously down a leather-clad leg. Simon falls to the ground, growling like a tiger while a spike heel crushes a rose. In the end, everyone is happily dancing as flower petals fall from above.

"HUNGRY LIKE THE WOLF"

This is the video that made it all happen for Duran Duran. A white-suited Simon in dark glasses sits in a restaurant deep in the heart of Sri Lanka. Looking desperate, he raises his dark glasses to look into the camera. He is surrounded by snake charmers and small Indian children. Meanwhile, John, Nick and Roger race through the market place looking for Simon. In slow motion, Simon overturns his table, scattering plates, silverware and water. He pushes through the crowded restaurant and into the street. In a clever page-turning effect, Simon is suddenly in the jungle. Dressed in

characteristic khakis, he is hunting down the el-
lusive beauty of his tortured reverie. The mysterious woman is seen in flashes behind trees,
in the market place, behind a rock. She's a
cross between a wild tiger and a woman. John
and Roger are still searching for Simon. They
question one of the local children and show
him a picture. Back in the jungle, Simon is cutting through brush, crossing treacherous
wooden bridges, wading through green lakes.
He's on "the hunt." Ultimately woman and
man meet. Nose to nose, eye to eye. They embrace, they tumble in the grass, they struggle.
Moans of joy (terror? excitement?) are heard.
Simon raises his face and reveals claw marks
on his neck. He's suddenly back in the restaurant. Was he dreaming? Was he remembering?
The claw marks are intact. John, Nick and
Roger finally find Simon seated at his table.
Happy to see him, they gather around the table
and talk. The song fades, the image fades, the
video ends.

"NIGHTBOAT"

This eerie and frightening clip features more
role-playing on the part of the band. Band,
crew and director return to the island of Antigua, but this time not for fun in the sun. The

video begins at an abandoned boathouse. Andy and Nick ride across the water in a little motorboat. Nick peers silently through a slatted window. Simon, sitting on the pier, whispers: "She'll be here soon . . . if she comes. Who is she? She is the fairy's midwife." He continues to murmur the mysterious passage. A mirror cracks when John gazes into it. As twilight settles in, John is taken over by a mysterious force. He screams and falls to the ground. With the darkness comes a host of horrifying ghouls that tear at and haunt all members of the band except Simon who is glimpsed singing on board the mysterious nightboat. The ghosts chase Andy and Roger into an abandoned house. In the end, a zombielike Nick stares on board the ship. Only Roger is left on the island wondering what happened to everybody else. The ghostly ship sails out over the dark water. Eerie . . .

"GIRLS ON FILM"

"Girls on Film" was one of the first X-rated videos ever made. Directed by the excellent directorial team of Kevin Godley and Lol Creme, the clip was very heavily edited before appearing on MTV. It can be seen on the *Duran Duran* video LP and the Duran Duran

Sony 45 in its uncut and uncensored version.

As the band plays in the background, we see the set being put together: Props are hauled about, technicians load cameras, sound equipment is checked. A bevy of beautiful models arrive one by one. Everyone is made up, hair coiffed and sprayed, costumes donned. In a humorous moment, Nick Rhodes whips out what looks like a switch blade. He ejects it and it's only a comb.

Using a boxing ring as the center stage, the scantily clad models parade before the cameras performing a series of erotic and sensual scenes. Two beauties perched upon a red-and-white candy-striped pole have a pillow fight. To remove the clinging pillow feathers from their bodies they pour glasses of champagne all over themselves. A mini-skirted nurse gives an oily massage to a burly patient. A real sumo wrestler is tossed about the ring by a small, lovely Asian girl who bows politely as she leaves the stage. A long-haired, slender beauty is drowning in a little kiddy pool; a heroic lifeguard attempts to save her. His mouth-to-mouth resuscitation turns into heavy kissing. She leaves him drowning in the same little pool. The clip concludes with a sexy mud wrestling scene. One of the wrestlers takes a refreshing shower before exiting the stage. Girls on film indeed.

"SAVE A PRAYER"

Spectacular scenes of Buddhist temples and the lush scenery of Sri Lanka characterize this solemn and meditative video clip. Simon sits alone in a room, singing quietly as the camera moves in slowly for a tight shot. The scene cuts to a beautiful beach with waves rushing in. Small Indian children dance and play in the sand and among the boats while the local men fish. John strums an acoustic guitar while Simon roams the beach observing the action. Scenes from the "Lonely in Your Nightmare" video flash across the screen. Simon dances with a lady. She abruptly leaves and he is alone on the empty dance floor. In the jungle, John and Nick play amidst the elephants and Roger swims in the clear blue water. As the final chorus rings, "Save a prayer for the morning after," all of the band members walk slowly toward a gigantic stone temple. As they arrive at the foot of the temple, they raise their heads and gaze at the sky. The scene returns to the opening shot of Simon singing alone. The music fades.

"THE CHAUFFEUR"

"The Chauffeur" is a step away from the

Duran Duran videos we have seen up to this point. The band does not appear at all. There are no strikingly beautiful beaches or temples or lush jungles. Instead we have a peculiar clip, directed by Ian Eames, about a mysterious chauffeur who drives two odd women dressed in undergarments to a provocative rendezvous in an empty garage of sorts. One woman applies makeup in a room surrounded by beveled mirrors while the other rides in the back of the big car. The ominous chauffeur appears on and off in the background. When the women finally meet, they take part in a strange dance while the chauffeur watches. This clip is similar to "Nightboat," but without the phantoms.

"IS THERE SOMETHING I SHOULD KNOW"

This video is very much the grand finale of the show as it closes out this innovative video LP. Directed once again by Mulcahy, the video is a rehash of where the band has been and a foreshadowing, perhaps, of where they are going. The song was released as a single after the success of the *Rio* LP and was a prelude to *Seven and the Ragged Tiger*. The oft-repeated chorus of "Please, please tell me now, is there something I should know?" can be interpreted as a request from the band to their audience to determine the future success of Duran Duran. The band is dressed uniformly in blue shirts, dark pants and light-colored ties tucked into their shirts. An exercise in video editing, the clip is characterized by split screens and short cuts edited in perfect tempo with the upbeat tune. Geometry is a theme here: The band sings perched upon squares and triangles; John plays with a mathematical device; Simon appears in multiple images walking through a maze of circles and squares and straight lines. Intercut with all this geometry are scenes of a little boy running through a forest carrying a big red ball. He is chased by a small crowd while Simon watches curiously from behind the barren trees. Also intercut are cryptic scenes in black and white of businessmen stepping out from behind stone columns reading newspapers. Flashes of previous videos pass by reminding us that the past is gone and a new phase is being entered. This is not the end, it seems to be saying, but a pause in the action. And it won't be long before there will be even more exciting visual images and music from Duran Duran, the video golden boys.

1983-84 did indeed bring just that from Duran Duran. With the release of *Seven and the Ragged Tiger*, in the latter part of 1983, came three new videos from the genre's forerunners. It goes without saying that the songs which these videos were accompanying became smash hits worldwide. Let's take a closer look at "New Moon on Monday," "Union of the Snake" and "The Reflex."

"NEW MOON ON MONDAY"

"Ladies and gentlemen," announces the white-faced emcee on an empty stage in a large theater. He begins speaking in French as the camera pans back and we see Simon sitting in the theater. A sultry, dark-haired woman dressed in black is the only other person watching the small troupe of actors that have taken the stage. She turns her attention to Simon and gives an usher, who is suddenly standing by, a message to give to him. She leaves. Simon slowly descends a dark stairway which leads to a back alley. He dons a helmet and joins the mysterious lady on her motorcycle. They ride down a desolate cobblestone street. The action cuts to Nick and John loading boxes labeled "explosives" onto a horse-drawn carriage. Roger finds Andy at an old-fashioned printing press making small leaflets. They are preparing for some kind of happening—but what is it?

Simon and the young lady ride across the European countryside until they arrive in the town where John, Nick, Andy and Roger await them. They all gather around a table in a secluded restaurant, seemingly to solidify plans for the coming events.

In an open town square, the Durans hand out the leaflets. They remove them from inside their jackets and quietly slip them to villagers passing by. As night falls, Andy and Roger run through the darkened streets carrying a giant kite which they send flying against a blackened sky. Nick and John unload the boxes from the carriage and break them open with axes. Simon comes running down the street with the lady from the theater waving a big yellow flag. The square fills with people and military men on white horses. A bonfire is lit while everyone begins to dance and sing. As Simon sings: "I light my torch and sing," everyone is suddenly waving a flaming torch or a sparkler, and colorful fireworks begin to shoot into the sky and explode all around them. The chorus rings out: "New moon on Monday and a fire dance through the night/I stayed the cold day with a lonely satellite," as all the band members and crowds of people dance and sing enthusiastically beneath the fireworks.

"UNION OF THE SNAKE"

"Union of the Snake" is perhaps the most

unusual video Duran Duran have appeared in to date. Characterized by vast desert terrains, hot sun, mysterious underground caverns and dancing lizardlike creatures, it is difficult to discern the plot of this video, if there is one.

In the beginning, John, Simon and Roger are walking across a sun-beaten desert dune. As night falls, they find an abandoned pick-up truck with a body in it. He is presumably dead. John and Roger are suddenly overtaken and pass out. A surprised Simon is approached by a beautiful girl dressed in a red, hotel bellhop suit. She beckons him to come with her. An elevator appears on the sand and she and Simon descend into an underground cavern. The underground hide-out opens into a large, ornately decorated corridor. Two huge wooden doors are opened and Simon enters. We see Nick hunched over a secret map. He mouths the words: "I got it," then he carefully rolls up the map and places it into a black tube. Andy is seen scurrying through a smoky room filled with children and scantily clad dancers. He climbs a large scaffolding and is out of sight. Simon panics and attempts to escape the unusual and frightening place. He crawls out from a tube which leads him back to John and Roger who have regained consciousness and have been looking for Simon. From over the hill, bright, colorful fireworks begin to fill the sky around them. Simon approaches the source of the fireworks only to be struck down. He falls in slow motion and rolls down the sandy dune.

It is morning and Simon wakes up on the sand. He looks around as if he can't determine whether he was dreaming or it was real. He looks around him. He finds the black tube containing the map. It was real. A robed man on horseback rides up and offers Simon his arm. They lock arms and Simon is whisked up into the saddle and together they ride off across the sand.

"THE REFLEX"

"The Reflex" is a performance video shot during Duran Duran's recent world tour. Although it is a performance video, it is still filled with the unique characteristics of a Duran Duran clip. A scrambled TV screen clears and reveals the Duran Duran backup singers ready for action. As the camera pans back, we see that we are watching a huge video screen perched high above the stage where Duran Duran are ready to perform. As the music begins, John, Andy and Simon jump (literally) into action.

The audience is tremendous. Thousands of

Duran Duran fans are seen singing, dancing, clapping hands and even crying over this thrilling event. The action switches from Simon's strutting and dancing about the stage, Andy leaping around and strumming his guitar, John coolly playing his sax, sultry Nick behind his keyboard and a frenetic Roger beating his drums to images on the video screen of shadowy figures dancing and couples embracing. At times the action on the stage is the same as the image on the screen. The highlight of this video is an animated waterfall that springs forth from the giant video screen and splashes the surprised and shocked audience below.

This clip is a fine performance video in that it strays from the usual performance fare by integrating the onstage video screen and includes a lot of audience participation.

Most of the Duran Duran videos have been the work of Australia-born director Russell Mulcahy. Mulcahy has been called "the uncrowned king of video rock," responsible for turning many of the music industry's hottest stars into three-minute film heroes. Aside from Duran Duran, Mulcahy has directed an endless stream of rockers including Spandau Ballet ("True"), Billy Joel ("Allentown" and "Pressure"), Fleetwood Mac ("Gypsy") and Asia

("Heat of the Moment"). Russell has been the recipient of numerous awards including a special BAFTA Craft awards for his contributions to the music promotion business; and, the American Television Awards named Mulcahy's video for Rod Stewart, "Young Turks," as best video, as well as naming Mulcahy best director.

A Russell Mulcahy video is characterized by a deep understanding of the group and their music as well as a fine comprehension of the medium. Mulcahy realized quickly that the video explosion is one of the most important trends in rock & roll history. Today, image is as important as sound. "Because of videos there is a whole new breed of rock stars who have to be actors as well as performers," says the director. "Duran Duran are very good indeed, particularly Simon Le Bon, who is a natural."

And it makes perfect sense that Simon would be a natural on video. He spent many years (from early childhood until he became lead singer for Duran Duran) studying professional acting. Simon was always fascinated by the stage and was always a "show off" (his words) in high school. As the lyricist for the band, Simon has an uncanny ability to create a distinct persona for the songs. That insight combined with his acting ability enables Simon to portray those characters with great prowess on video.

91

A perfectionist, Mulcahy admits that he is often not pleased with the finished product and can see how the clip could have been better. However, he is quite pleased and proud of the work he's done with Duran Duran. His finely directed videos of "Hungry Like the Wolf" and "Rio" were two of the most important elements in propelling Duran Duran into superstardom. That is an achievement he can be very proud of.

Russell Mulcahy's career began as a film director for Channel Seven in his homeland of Australia. After editing news and documentaries, Russell began to write, direct, and edit short films of his own. In 1976 and 1977 he won awards at the Sydney Film Festival in the short film category. The prize money from these awards helped Mulcahy leave Channel Seven and set up a production company in Australia to produce rock & roll promotional films and other musical specials.

In 1978, Mulcahy went to England to film a punk band, intending to stay for a month. He never returned to Australia. He joined Jon Roseman Production, England's leading promo company at the time. After two years, Mulcahy joined forces with two other leading video directors, Lexi Godfrey and David Mallet, to form MGM, their own production company. It ran successfully for a year and a half. Their only serious competitors were Brian Grant and Scott Millaney. Well, if you can't beat 'em, join 'em. Mulcahy and Mallet merged with their competitors to form a new company— MGMM. This partnership proved very successful resulting in major overseas opportunities, and a great deal of recognition for the directors.

Since 1982, Russell has been making rock videos with major stars all over the world. Although he plans to continue his work in this field, he has been considering many scripts and ideas for feature films. The latest rumor is that Mulcahy will be returning to Australia to work on his first feature film, currently titled *Razorback*.

It makes sense that a very special group like Duran Duran would choose such a special director to make the videos that have been so important to their careers thus far. Duran Duran takes music video very seriously—not only as promotional tools, but as a serious art form and an extension of their creative powers.

The exotic locales chosen for several of the Duran Duran videos were the decision of both the director and the band. As John Taylor remembers: "We decided it was time to get back to nature, so there we were with elephants, jungles, cameramen, video crew, dancers and makeup department." Choosing such out-of-the-way places as Sri Lanka was not without its problems. Roger Taylor nearly suffered a fatal accident during the filming of "Save a Prayer." While riding an elephant during one scene, the elephant began to charge down the river after another elephant. Roger managed to jump off just before the two huge animals collided. As Roger recalls: "It was one of the most frightening experiences of my life." Fortunately, no one was hurt. Crowd control has also been a problem on the set, especially in Sri Lanka. Mulcahy remembers that during the film of "Hungry Like the Wolf," the cast and crew had to rely on armed police to control the onlookers.

The work Duran Duran has done with Russell Mulcahy has been stunning. They are some of the finest videos ever to cross the TV screen. The Durans, as Mulcahy has said and as anyone could easily recognize, are video naturals— they have style, grace, and acting talent as well as musical talent. The success of their videos has established Duran Duran as pop music trendsetters and musical superstars.

7. Duranomania Sweeps Across America

Duran Duran played their first American tour back in 1981 after the release in the U.K. of the single "Planet Earth," and after their first headlining tour of Great Britain. At first, the response in America to the new British invaders was not exactly overwhelming. American audiences seemed slow to pick up on the excitement Duran Duran had been generating among rock-loving Britons. By the time the American and U.K. tours were over, "Planet Earth" had risen to an impressive number two on the U.K. charts while in the U.S. it had only just made its way onto the playlists of some of the more progressive dance clubs in New York as an import.

Later on in that year the first packaging of their debut LP hit the charts. Simply called *Duran Duran*, the album immediately solidified the popularity of the band all across England— the LP soared to the number two spot. Their second single, "Girls on Film," from the same LP, shot to the number five spot. At that point Duran Duran began to receive some much deserved airplay on new music radio stations here in the States. The accompanying promotional video for "Girls on Film" was seen on what was then a new cable music video network, MTV— now a music business phenomenon. The version of the clip that made it to the air was heavily edited. The original version contained much nudity, and the tape was stamped "too saucy" for American eyes.

Following the success of *Duran Duran* and "Girls on Film," the band embarked on a second headlining tour of the U.K. By the end of 1981, Duran Duran had progressed from local heroes to national pop stars.

In 1982 Duran Duran set their sights not only on America, but also the world. The first stop was the exotic isle of Sri Lanka (formerly Ceylon). The band took a hiatus here in the tropics to work on three of their most exciting promotional videos. Little did they know at the

Once upon a time even the stars of Duran Duran were little boys. This is Nick Rhodes (formerly Nick Bates) as a lad in Birmingham, England. (Photo: Syndication International—PHOTO TRENDS)

Who would have guessed that this young lad, fly undone and swinging by his arms, would turn into a superstar? This is John Taylor in the garden of his parents' home in May 1967. John was home with the German measles. (Photo: Syndication International—PHOTO TRENDS)

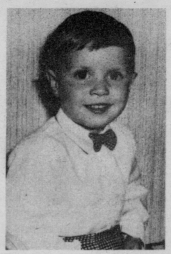

A wide-eyed and innocent Simon Le Bon as a little boy (Photo: Syndication International—PHOTO TRENDS)

Duran Duran with their look of the eighties. Left to right: Andy Taylor, John Taylor, Simon Le Bon, Roger Taylor and Nick Rhodes.

Duran Duran

Simon Le Bon and Nick Rhodes discuss the music of Duran Duran with the press during one of the group's many press conferences. (Photo: John Bellissimo)

Gorgeous John Taylor enjoys a drink and a smoke at a post-concert party in California. (Photo: John Bellissimo)

Roger Taylor backstage at a post-concert party
(Photo: John Bellissimo)

Andy Taylor during a recent press interview
(Photo: John Bellissimo)

Nick Rhodes (Photo: John Bellissimo)

Capitol Records held a special private party for Duran Duran when they were presented with a gold record for their *Rio* LP. Pictured here from left to right: Andy Taylor, Bruce Garfield (vice president in charge of Artist Relations, Capitol Records), Roger Taylor and John Taylor. (Photo: John Bellissimo)

At the same party Duran Duran proudly display their gold LPs. Pictured with the band is the president of Capitol Records, Jim Mazza (center), and one of the Duran's managers Paul Berrow (in background). (Photo: John Bellissimo)

When Duran Duran made a special in-store
appearance at New York's 49th street Video Shack
outlet, everybody wanted an autograph—even the
babies. (Photo: John Bellissimo)

On stage at New York's Madison Square Garden,
Simon Le Bon jams with Nile Rogers (a member of
Chic). Nile will be producing Duran Duran's next
studio LP.

The students of Mark Twain Junior high school were the winners of a special contest held to raise money for the American Olympic Team. As the lucky winners, the school received a visit from Duran Duran. Pictured here are members of the school's administration and students with Duran Duran.

Andy Warhol joins Duran members Nick Rhodes and Simon Le Bon at SIR studios in New York (where NBC's *Saturday Night Live* is done) to tape an interview for Warhol's cable TV program. (Photo: John Bellissimo)

John Taylor and Simon Le Bon have some fun on stage during their Madison Square Garden performance. (Photo: John Bellissimo)

At a *Saturday Night Live* season wrap up party held at New York's Trax, the members of Duran Duran partied with friends and family. Pictured left to right: Claire Stansfield (Simon's girlfriend), Simon Le Bon, Simon's mother Ann, Nick Rhodes and his girl friend Juliana Friedman. (Photo: John Bellissimo)

Backstage at Madison Square Garden Simon Le Bon is greeted by MTV Veejays Martha Quinn, J.J. Jackson and Nina Blackwood. (Photo: John Bellissimo)

Duran Duran were the musical guests on the popular late night TV show *Saturday Night Live* in 1983. (Photo: John Bellissimo)

time that one video would catapult them to the ranks of international superstars. "Hungry Like the Wolf," "Lonely in Your Nightmare" and "Save a Prayer" were the three clips done in this land that has become synonymous with Duran Duran. The songs would appear later on the band's second LP, *Rio*.

Meanwhile, "Planet Earth" rose to the number one spot on the Australian record charts. The group followed up with an early 1982 tour Down Under, followed by Japan. For the first time, Duran Duran found themselves besieged by young female fans. It was suddenly necessary to travel with police escorts in order to keep the adoring fans at bay. Critics were quick to recognize the similarities between Duran Duran in 1982 and the Beatles in 1964. There were many casual similarities: Both groups hail from small English towns — (Duran Duran from Birmingham and the Beatles from Liverpool: both record for the same record label — Capitol. But members of the band acknowledge only one thing they truly share with John, Paul, George and Ringo: the ability to make girls *scream*. Even keyboardist Nick Rhodes comments, "The hysterical crowd reaction we get is probably similar to what the Beatles got." Not that they would remember since most of the members of this band were only one or two years old at the time the Beatles were making rock & roll history.

As the 1982 tour continued, Duran Duran's second LP, *Rio*, was released worldwide. The album jumped to the number two spot on the British charts. It immediately went platinum in Australia (over one million copies sold). American DJs, however, were not impressed. Duran Duran received little airplay this side of the Atlantic.

Then the single "Hungry Like the Wolf" hit the American music market, blitzing the U.S. radio stations, in June. MTV caught Duran Duran fever and began to show the accompanying video. Reaction to the clip was unprecedented. "Hungry Like the Wolf" became an enormous hit. Duran Duran had finally snagged America.

The group's second assault on North America came that summer. Duran Duran performed thirty-four concerts, twenty-five as headliners and nine as support act for the rock group, Blondie, in arenas reaching from six hundred to forty thousand people. U.S. radio stations were forced to yield to the newest wave of the British invasion and Duran Duran's music came to the fore.

During the months of September and October of 1982, Duran Duran continued their attack on the world by touring Europe and including shows in Norway, Sweden, Finland,

Denmark, France, Germany, Holland and Belgium. This was followed by another twenty-four date, sold-out headline tour of the U.K. which included a date at the prestigious Hammersmith Odeon. In between the *Duran Duran* and the *Rio* LPs, Capitol also released *Carnival*, a four-song mini LP featuring extended dance versions of "Girls on Film," "Hungry Like the Wolf," "Hold Back the Rain" and "My Own Way." The extended versions were re-mixed by David Kershenbaum in the United States and were only a part of this special, limited-edition LP, which has since been deleted from the catalogue.

Meanwhile, back in the U.S., Capitol Records decided to re-mix the *Rio* LP and re-service it to radio stations and journalists. The response was astonishing. Almost six months after its original release, *Rio* exploded onto the charts. A new version of "Hungry Like the Wolf" was released as a single in December and promptly zoomed to the number three position. The single "Rio" also attained the number three spot. The now multi-platinum selling album has since settled at number six. Overnight the world was overtaken by what the hip British press is calling "Fab Five Fever" or "Durandamonium."

In the interm of all these albums and singles making headline news, Duran Duran headed for the Caribbean, to the island of Antigua, to film two more videos with Russell Mulcahy (who directed the Sri Lankan clips). These were "Rio," which of course was the title tune of the album, and an eerie number called "Nightboat," which was really off the regular dance-romance trail that the band's music had been following. The clip came complete with gore-film ghouls and mysterious phantasms.

Hot on the heels of both "Rio" and "Hungry Like the Wolf," Duran Duran recorded a new single "Is There Something I Should Know," produced by Ian Little and Duran Duran. A toe-tapping, catchy little tune, "Is There Something I Should Know" became the Durans' eighth single in England. It entered the charts at the number one spot in early 1983, giving Duran Duran their first taste of life at the very top of the charts. A few weeks later, the single was released, in both seven- and twelve-inch versions, in the U.S. Of course the song was accompanied by yet another dazzling Russell Mulcahy video clip. The track quickly jumped to the number four spot on the *Billboard* and *Cashbox* charts.

"Is There Something I Should Know" was added to the *Duran Duran* package when it was re-mixed and repackaged for release in the United States complete with new sound and new photos. The original English version of the

100

LP is no longer in print and will probably become a valuable collector's item among those lucky Britons who bought it early on. This all-new *Duran Duran* LP went to number ten on the American charts after its rerelease, with about one million copies sold.

In July of 1983 Duran Duran received a great honor in their homeland when they played a concert at the Dominion Theater in Heathrow, England. This may have been the most important concert of the group's career because in attendance were Prince Charles and Princess Diana. After the performance the Princess announced that Duran Duran was one of her favorite groups and gave the band and the performance her royal seal of approval. Both Prince and Princess stayed late after the performance and attended a reception for the band.

Since video was the catalyst for the success of this energetic band of romantic rockers, it was logical that Duran Duran was among the first to release a full-length video cassette album (released by Thorn-EMI Video).

The next LP by Duran Duran was released at the end of 1983 and was called *Seven and the Ragged Tiger*. The album was recorded during a working holiday for the band in Montserrat, France. It went gold upon its release in the U.S. The first single off the album was "Union of the Snake," which was rush released in October of '83 in both seven-inch and twelve-inch formats. The song cracked the top ten on the American charts only a few weeks after its release and attained the number three spot in Britain after only three weeks. The follow-up single to "Union" was a tune called "New Moon on Monday" and it experienced the same kind of tremendous chart success as its predecessors. Both "Union of The Snake" and a third single released from the album, "The Reflex," were supported by elaborate new videos which quickly dominated the MTV playlist as well as the network show like *Friday Night Videos.*

Seven and the Ragged Tiger is considered a somewhat different album for Duran Duran. "It's a concept album of sorts," says Simon Le Bon. "It's an adventure story about a little commando team. The Seven is for us—the five band members and our two managers (Paul and Michael Berrow)—and The Ragged Tiger is success. It's ambition. That's what it's about."

Duran Duran's 1983-84 tour began in November of 1983 in Australia with a fan reception unmatched by any other band of similar stature. From Australia, it was off to Europe—all in a month's time before they returned to the U.K. to greet their home audience. In December of 1983, the U.K. tour culminated with five shows at the Wembley Arena. Duran Duran came to the United States in January of 1984 to play the largest arenas (to hold those very *large* crowds).

As Simon said, success and ambition is what it's all about. Success and ambition — that's what these five Birmingham rockers have. Are they here to stay? Ambition and drive like theirs is not easy to quell. And in view of their rapid-fire successes and their millions of steadfast followers, how could they go wrong?

8. The Duran Duran Sound

Night Music. That's what the members of Duran Duran have chosen to call their particular brand of pop music. But just what is night music? Music that you can enjoy during a night on the town might be the best way to explain the sound that Duran Duran have created. It's the kind of music that when it comes over the speakers at your favorite club you suddenly sit up and take notice. It defies people to remain seated—you just have to dance. And it's totally entertaining. The music is melodic, yet filled with so much energy and rhythm that it sets your body moving almost automatically.

Duran Duran do not like to be labeled as any one musical genre. It's considered a sure death for a musician to be linked to a single movement in terms of their continuing success. If an artist develops a reputation as being strictly "new wave" or "new romantic," it allows the artist little room for growth as a musical entity. Duran Duran would prefer their music move from strength to strength, following in its own natural and creative direction.

The musical sound of Duran Duran was carefully and methodically developed by the group's founders Nick Rhodes and John Taylor. It was their idea to combine disco (to inspire dance), rock, and rhythm & blues to make a new, sophisticated brand of dance music. Both John and Nick were greatly influenced by the American R & B group, Chic and the English art-rock band, Roxy Music. If you listen to any of the Duran Duran LPs, these influences become very apparent.

In the same way that disco encourages dance, so does the music of Duran Duran. In fact, John has described the Duran sound as "white, European disco." But whereas disco was generally lacking strong melody lines, the Durans have returned to a heavily melodic sound, something that has been absent from music in the past few years. The punk era, which preceded Duran Duran's popularity, was filled with hard, abrasive sounds which lacked real rhythms. Punk was more concerned with its political messages than with being mellifluous or entertaining. The music was brash and atonal. The Duran sound is tuneful and lyrical, filled with a gentle timbre—sweeter to the ear.

Another important quality of the music is that it is entertaining and accessible to their audience. Duran Duran is not out to be avant-garde. It was never their idea to leave the audience hanging under a cloud of mystery. Consequently, the band's rhythms are always contemporary, yet with an innovative edge that makes the music unique.

Each member of Duran Duran has contributed a great deal of thought to the making of the Duran Duran sound. The groundwork for each album is carefully planned in advance along with the band's producer. When the band enters the studio for a recording session, they know exactly what they want on tape and will not leave until they achieve it. With each new album the Duran Duran sound has progressed: It benefits from its influences, while becoming something of and unto itself as the musicians develop, learn and clarify their musical ideas.

The Duran Duran debut LP, simply titled *Duran Duran*, was filled with electric rhythms, which enhanced the air of mystery present in many of the album's cuts. Songs like "Planet Earth" and "(Waiting for the) Nightboat" have an almost celestial quality both lyrically and musically. In "Planet Earth," for instance, the synthesizers whine and drone in the background against the very steady bass lines and percussion beat. Simon's vocals occasionally linger on a particular line adding particular emphasis to words like "Can you hear me now/ There's no sign of life," making the song sound desperate as well as spacey and haunting. A diffused backing chorus of "This is planet earth, planet earth, planet earth," which fades out eerily as the heavy bass line takes over, only serves to add to the unearthy quality.

In a similar vein, "Nightboat" is a particularly eerie song on this first album. The song begins with a very haunting, almost supernatural-sounding synthesizer trill which sets the mood for this cryptic tune. The introduction builds to a rousing climax with a deep-rooted, frenzied bass line coupled with slow and moaning guitar riffs. In a hushed and deep voice, Simon sings of the mysterious "nightboat," embellishing his lyric with an occasional shout or cry as the song builds to a climatic ending.

"The Sound of Thunder," another song on the LP, was a tune Simon wrote to commemorate his acceptance into the band after his audition back at the Rum Runner. The lyrics reflect the band's excitement and eagerness to experience making music together. Lines like: "And I'm lying here/ that's what I was meant for/ waiting for the sound of thunder." Since Simon was the last member of Duran Duran to be inducted, it's a particularly moving song which speculates about the years to come and the band's positive attitude concerning their sure-fire success. The song seems to say that Duran Duran knew at this point that their formula was complete, that the future did indeed hold much success for them. But the song is in no way pompous or arrogant. It's a thoughtful chronicle of their humble beginnings, of their hopes and dreams for the future.

The highlight of this collection of tunes is probably "Girls on Film," which was a smash single for Duran Duran in 1981. The song opens with the sound of a camera motor drive being fired and the film advancing. The song really shows off Andy's funky and fancy guitar riffs and Roger's intense percussion. The lyrics are provocative and sexy: "The fuse is pumping heat is melting out on the wire/Give me shutters and whispers take me up to a shooting star."

By this time the Duran Duran sound was developing at a rapid pace. Evidence of this came with the release of the group's second LP, *Rio*, which was released in 1982 and produced by

Colin Thurston. The theme of the *Rio* LP seemed to be, "Let's dance!" Almost every cut on the disc is filled with a bouncy melody and an infectious tune. *Rio* is also a very romantic album. From the opening cut on side one, in which Simon sings the joyous praises to a beautiful girl named Rio, to the mournful and tender "Lonely in Your Nightmare," where the chorus repeats the desperate and loving plea of "You're lonely in your nightmare, let me in," the album is filled with warm images of love and romance and appears to pay homage to that special relationship between a man and a woman.

A spectacular cut on the LP is "Save a Prayer." The song has become a concert favorite among Duran Duran fans as its solemn, mounting chorus of "Save a prayer till the morning after, save a prayer till the morning after," inspires great audience participation. "Save a Prayer" contains some of the group's most beautiful lyrics.

> *Pretty looking road I try to hold the rising*
> *floods that fill my skin*
> *Don't ask me why I'll keep my promise*
> *melt the ice*
> *And you wanted to dance, so I asked you*
> *to dance but a fear was in your soul.*

Rio also contained the most famous Duran Duran single to date, "Hungry Like the Wolf." This song represented the turning point in Duran Duran's career as it was the song that turned them from English stars to international superstars. And it's no wonder — it is a very special song indeed. It's a fine example of just how catchy and infectious Duran Duran's music can be. The tune is memorable and easy to get caught up in. The vocals are superbly delivered and enhanced by moaning and sighing as well as whispers and heavy breathing. The song is about a man on the hunt for passion and love. The vivid images are those of dark city nights, full moons rising, hearts beating and mouths watering. "Hungry Like the Wolf" is a very sexy and seductive song which probably had a lot to do with its success.

Overall, *Rio* has a tighter construction than the *Duran Duran* album which preceded it. It has more of a thematic concept and a stronger musical direction. Producer Colin Thurston did a fine job of capturing the growing instrumental prowess of this relatively new group, using it to its best advantage. Nick's synthesizer is wistful and elegant and fills each tune with a rich, full-bodied and lush sound. John's bass is always deep and rhythmical, while Roger and Andy nicely fill the gaps and keep the melody moving quickly along.

A Duran Duran album never sounds over-produced. Never does the music drown out the vocal dub. The mix is always designed to place as much emphasis as possible on the melody and the lyric. This was a particularly fine feature of the *Rio* LP.

The end of 1983 brought Duran Duran's most recent album release, *Seven and the Ragged Tiger*. This LP is no doubt the group's finest recorded achievement to date. Simon Le Bon described *Seven and the Ragged Tiger* as a concept album of sorts, which makes it a departure from the band's usual fare. A concept album is one that has a theme running throughout. In this LP the *Seven* represents the five band members and their two managers, Paul and Michael Berrow. *The Ragged Tiger* is a symbol of the success they fought so furiously for and finally attained.

The album opens with Duran Duran's most recent hit single, "The Reflex." This song seems to be about Duran Duran's quest for success and their theory that as individuals we are in control of our own destinies. Simon sings:

The Reflex is an only child he's waiting in the park
The Reflex is in charge of finding treasure in the dark
And watching over lucky clover isn't that

bizarre
Every little thing the Reflex does leaves
  you answered with a ?

The reflex is a symbol of the control a person has over the future. It waits alone like an unknowing child to be found and have its talents triggered. When it is discovered, it can reveal hidden treasures and secrets. In comparison to the Reflex, simple daydreaming and wishing ("watching over lucky clover") without taking action is absurd and bizarre. The song's chorus is a determined plea by the singer to use the resources available.

> *Why don't you use it*
> *Try not to bruise it*
> *Buy time don't lose it*

This song perfectly sums up what Duran Duran are all about — the secret of their success and happiness. It's no wonder it has been such a tremendous success with the group's fans.

Another interesting track on the *Seven and the Ragged Tiger* LP is "Shadows on Your Side." This song appears to be Duran Duran's homage to their fans. The song outlines both the negative and positive aspects of being public figures. "Shackled and raised for a shining crowd . . . All of their roar with the heat of the planet's core," the song begins. The first chorus talks about the constancy of the public in an entertainer's life.

> *The shadows are on your side*
> *As soon as the lights go down*
> *In the darkest places you can find*
> *You belong to the hands of the night*

Your public remains in your mind and heart even when you're alone (the shadows are on your side), the song seems to say. As a performer, you belong to your public and must live for their approval and their applause (The hands of the night). But the second part of the song tells the listener that sometimes the constant support of the loyal following and the confidence an artist derives from that is often comforting and needed.

> *Spinning a compass to choose your way*
> *You can run you can dive you can stand*
> *you can soar*
> *Whichever way you can be sure that*
> *The shadows are on your side.*

The song reminds us that the true loyalty of an artist's fans remains with a celebrity no matter what he chooses to do. Their public (at least Duran Duran's public) has come to accept them for exactly what they are and the freedom to expand as artists is always there.

Duran Duran's lyrics are a very important element of the band's sound and are a sign of the band's continuing development as artists. They are not average pop lyrics by any means. There are not very many simple tales of boy meets girl, boy loses girl. Lyricist Simon Le Bon is very much a rock & roll poet, in the same vein as Joni Mitchell or Kris Kristofferson. The often brooding, speculative lyrics probe into the universe which surrounds us. Lyrics like these suggest that the life of a superstar is not always what it seems. The joy of living is often overshadowed by fears and confusion and also pain. The lyrics seem to be specifically designed to make the listener contemplate. They are certainly not meant to be depressing, but rather they are meant to provoke curiosity and wonder. Duran Duran's artistry lies in their ability to fuse lyrics that make you think to music that makes you dance.

The music of Duran Duran is still in its very early stages. These artists are rapidly maturing. They are highly charged and filled with inspiration all the time. As a band and as individual musicians, they have only begun to tap their talents. Surely the future will contain more of the famous Duran Duran night music, but more importantly, we can look forward to advances and innovations. Duran Duran will continue to write songs and move deeper and deeper into their souls to do it. Not only will they continue to make a lot of people happy with their brand of music, but they will come to fulfill themselves as creators and artists.

9. Behind the Glitter

The life of a rock & roll idol is filled with more fabulous moments than you or I could ever imagine. The star-studded moments of glamour, excitement, fulfillment and creative joy seem too much for only one lifetime. Not only can a rock star enjoy the powerful and triumphant hours on stage playing his music to thousands of adoring fans, but there are also the long hours in the recording studio when he is the almighty creator of the music that makes the world dance and sing. The music that people sing while they are working, shopping, or just walking down the street. The music that makes the world feel good.

Apart from actually making music, the life of a rock star is filled with an exciting array of extras. There are the parties, for instance, at the most fashionable places in the world like Area, Limelight, Studio 54 and the Ritz, just to mention a few in New York. Not only does the rock personality attend these parties, they are often the guest of honor!

And what about all the traveling! A famous musical personality visits virtually every major city in the world — London, Paris, Sydney, New York, Los Angeles, Tokyo, Rome and Hong Kong, to name a few. In every new place there are new and exciting people to be met, new adventures to be had. What could possibly be more wonderful than being a rock & roll superstar?

Well, try asking one. You might be surprised at the answer.

Being in the public eye is just not as fantastic as it all seems. After one concert, there's another, and yet another, sometimes only several hours apart. And then comes the exhaustion. As for the partying . . . often there are so many people hounding you there isn't time for a pleasant conversation or a friendly drink. And the traveling, well, of course it's enlightening to visit all those different cultures and exotic cities. But what about the lonely nights when it seem you are the only person who doesn't speak the language. Or what about when you pass through a city so quickly that the next day you barely remember where you were. And the fans, yes, they love you, but for every fan that loves you there are at least two that can't stand you or your band. And let's not forget the presence that haunts every personality in every genre of entertainment—the critic. Along with the critic comes the other hounding members of the press who stake their lives on their ability to uncover every shred of your life for a story.

What about all of that? On second thought, the life of a rock star may not be so enviable, after all.

Despite their enormous popularity and the generally happy attitude the band projects, things are not much different for Duran Duran. All the problems of being well-known rock personalities are there; it takes a huge amount of strength and perseverance on the parts of John, Nick, Simon, Andy and Roger to survive.

Success has undoubtedly brought its share of problems for the band. True, they can hardly complain about the devotion of their fans or their enormous record sales. But these are the same things that have caused them to become the butt of some very malicious criticism and often outlandish media speculation. Duran Duran have been repeatedly attacked for being sexist, shallow, and artistically worthless. They are also accused of being boringly heterosexual in this age of such androgenous personalities as Boy George, Annie Lennox and Michael Jackson. Also, the idea that Duran Duran is strictly for the teenybopper set is beginning to wear thin.

"The hardest thing for us to cop is the charge that we're artistically slight," said John Taylor to a reporter from *The Record* magazine. "That's something we've never understood. We have never done anything as blatantly commercial as 'Karma Chameleon' or 'True' and I don't think we've ever recorded anything as banal, but in the eyes of the media, we haven't got half the integrity of these groups. I suppose if we started getting good reviews, we might stop selling records, but it does niggle all the same," John concluded.

It's true. Although for the record buying public, the members of Duran Duran are the new gods of rock & roll, the record reviewers and industry honchos accuse them of being musically one step above the Monkees.

One English magazine reported: "The worst thing about their success is that they don't deserve a penny of it." This came after the reviewer saw one of the band's concerts in

Europe. Another reviewer said about the Duran Duran video LP: "Just what did Duran Duran—an unexceptional collection of pop pretties as vapid on stage as they are on record—have that deserves all this attention." Ouch!

The band, as well as many of their fans, feel that this kind of criticism is most definitely undeserved. John feels that at least part of the problem originated in England: "We've never been part of the social scene whereby we were mingling with *New Musical Express* reporters. I think if they knew us as people, and knew we were not put together by a record company, that we're genuine, they might not be so critical. We're not the shallow pop group that people think of us as. Although, we're undoubtedly a *pop* group. We *like* pop music, but as in Roxy's 'Virginia Plain,' not as in 'Karma Chameleon.' To me that's too obvious."

In order to gain more credibility as a rock & roll band and to play down the teenybopper image, Duran Duran's latest musical adventure, the *Seven and the Ragged Tiger* LP, was a very serious undertaking. The band had a lot to live up to—more smash singles than you could shake a stick at, one gold, and one platinum LP. They also had an upcoming world tour which would either make or break them on the stages of America (their most difficult proving ground). This album had to work. Together with producers Ian Little and Alex Sadkin, Duran Duran set up a very rigorous recording studio schedule. In the past they had always been a band that recorded quickly. With this crucial LP the band spent over six months recording and perfecting this product.

John remembers those tedious months in the studio: "It came as a bit of a shock when for the hundredth time, the producer was still asking you to try something again. You felt like screaming, 'What, again?' " But the band was determined to make this album the most perfect of their career. "We wanted an album we could live with for a long time," John continued. "One that countered the disposable image people seem to have of us and which we've been trying to shake off for some time." The band views the completed and successful *Seven* LP to be a massive development of their sound that transcends mere improvement. The album is a powerful example of the increasingly sophisticated Duran style. There is a new fluidity to the rhythms as well as a vast improvement in the production quality. The instrumentation shows great advancement in style and showmanship and, quite frankly, Le Bon's vocals have never sounded better. The increased time and effort spent on this LP is obvious, and will, one hopes, finally prove the artistic worth of Duran Duran.

Along with their breakthrough on MTV—and partly because of it—it is Duran Duran's irresistible "image" that is responsible for the pedestal on which they stand triumphantly today. Their stylish, glamour-boy image has also gotten them into some deep trouble. There is no doubt that Duran Duran and their managers, the Bellows, have spent an enormous amount of time *and* money in creating their very special appearance. But it's that same image that has tarnished the band's credibility as real rockers. The Durans do not feel that their look and style was strictly manufactured, or that it's anything to be ashamed of. They happen to really look like that. It's also true that the majority of people that attend a Duran Duran concert are young, screaming girls. It's also true that almost all of their fan mail is from women (many of which include X-rated photos, mostly from Americans). A significant point is that Andy's mail dropped off rather drastically when fans found out that he had gotten married. The problem: The only people who seem to take them seriously are members of the younger rock & roll crowd. As five adult men, this disturbs them.

Members of the band feel that beyond taking care of their natural good looks and dressing stylishly and comfortably, they have done nothing to encourage the "image as sale" theory, and that it is the media that foists a phony glamour-boy mystique upon the band. A simple case of misrepresentation. The tragic result of all this is that, though serious musicians, they are unable to attract a broader, more adult audience. There is no doubt that they love their younger fans, but they would like to have more mass appeal. John Taylor comments on the dilemma: "One of our biggest annoyances is that people seem scared or embarrassed to like Duran Duran or to come to one of our concerts. I find it a fairly alarming state of affairs when people are getting about saying, 'Don't tell anyone I said so, but I quite like Duran Duran.' I don't suppose there is a lot you can do about it. We've never tried to be teen-oriented. I never thought our lyrics were designed for only fifteen-year-olds.

The fact is: Duran Duran is not strictly a bubble-gum band. Behind the glitter, the desire to party and the fancy clothes are five mature musicians who take their professions very seriously. On the *Seven and the Ragged Tiger* LP you will not find the songs that traditionally appeal to the under-fifteen crowd. You won't find girl-meets-boy love songs that have made artists like Shaun Cassidy or even Rick Springfield teen idols. As a matter of fact, most of Duran Duran's lyrics are poetically cryptic and require some hard thinking. "Planet Earth," for instance, or "Union of the Snake." Again, John Taylor adamantly responds to the issue: "I really love those interviews with people like Pete Townshend where they ask him what he thinks of certain issues. Nobody asks *us* those questions. So they think we're unable to think on any other level than fourteen-year-old girls. While I instinctively don't want Duran Duran to be associated with any sort of political preaching, it'd be nice to talk about other things."

Final words on their image: Simon Le Bon firmly believes that the image Duran Duran presents in their music, in their looks and in their videos is a positive one. "It presents kids with a very obvious example of people who've done something to get out of the dumps. We've been called decadent. I don't agree. We are very optimistic. I don't think the world is crumbling. I think it's just a matter of people doing things themselves and not putting too much weight on the politicians' shoulders and letting them live your life for you. I believe in looking after myself. I think I do it better than anyone else does."

Traveling and touring have also caused their share of related problems for the Durans. Being on the road is hectic and exhausting. During the band's second American tour Andy even suffered a physical collapse which caused them to go off the road for a few days. And as much as all of the Duran's live for putting on the best possible show, they don't really like the actual rigors of touring. As Nick describes being on the road: "Getting up in the morning. Sixteen hours a day, when you're on tour, traveling every day, you don't get much sleep. I love playing the gigs, but I don't like traveling to the airport, waiting for the luggage and so on." But all this is nothing compared to the siege of fans that often invade the privacy (what little there is of it) of each band member when they arrive in town. The Durans have developed somewhat of a love-hate relationship with their fans these days. Certainly they can't thank them enough for their love, support, and out-and-out adoration. But the intrusion is getting to be a little too much to bear. As John put it after a particularly hectic day: "We've gotten to the point where we've had it for three years now and really don't enjoy it anymore. I almost get blasé about it now. You just want it to be kept at bay." For instance, while in New York earlier this year, Andy opened his closet door in his room at the Berkshire Place hotel where the band was staying and found three enthusiastic fans inside. Mobs of Duran Duran lovers waited behind police barricades when the band arrived at the hotel, many of whom had waited there for eight or nine hours. Needless to say, no place is sacred. Fans manage to find Duran Duran wherever they go.

Probably the most difficult thing to bear while on the road is being so far away from home and family and friends. All admit to this. Says John: "It's like a nightmare sometimes. I've got a flat in London that I've spent only ten nights in and I bought a house in the country that I've only been in once." Ironically, these are five guys who once couldn't afford such luxuries, and now that they can, they have no time to enjoy them.

The next time you aspiring young musicians think: "If only I could be famous," think twice. Or the next time you read about a legitimate band being criticized unnecessarily, maybe you should find out more before you believe it. Sure, being a celebrity is exciting—in some ways. But one must be prepared to accept the bitter with the sweet. The five men who make up Duran Duran are a special breed of entertainers. Mature beyond their years and driven by a tremendous ambition and desire, their goal in life is a simple one—to make great music. And these guys are not going to let anyone stand in their way.

10. Causing A Riot (Almost) on Broadway

Forty-ninth Street and Broadway is the throbbing heart of the bustling metropolis of New York City. Just about any time of the day or night the area is filled with hordes of active New Yorkers on their way somewhere. During the day you find them window shopping, lunching in the many restaurants, or visiting the unique novelty shops which overwhelm the area. Then, in the evening, you find movie-goers lined up for the latest flick in town (anything from *Friday the 13th* to Fellini's *The Ship Sails On* in this neighborhood or friends gathering for an early dinner of anything from

Burger King to Japanese cuisine. Of course the famous Times Square area attracts all sorts of tourists, especially on a Saturday night. Kids come in from the suburbs to hang out and take in the much-talked-about New York sites (including the strip of "skin flick" theaters along Forty-second Street) and the surrounding theater district brings out-of-towners in to see shows like *Cats*, *A Chorus Line* and *Zorba* on the world famous Broadway. The human tide is an everyday occurrence here.

If you happened to have been in New York last year, and just happened to walk down Forty-ninth Street, you would have seen a sight considered shocking to even a native New Yorker (and as a New Yorker I can verify that these people have seen some pretty shocking sights). What you would have seen that afternoon was five thousand New York youths, many carrying lavish bouquets and assorted gift boxes, crowded outside the iron gates of the Forty-ninth Street Video Shack outlet. The throngs of teenagers spilled over onto the sidewalks surrounding the Forty-ninth Street and Broadway entrance to the store and extended all the way down to Forty-eighth Street. What was the cause of this outrageous melee? Duran Duran was in town.

Video Shack, in conjunction with Capitol Records and the Sony Consumer Products Company, planned for the afternoon of March 19, a first-time-ever music artist in-store appearance. Duran Duran would appear to promote the Duran Duran video 45 which had just been released. The nearly riotous conditions which occurred, however, were not planned.

Put out by the Sony Corporation, the video 45 featured two songs by Duran Duran, both of which had been receiving heavy airplay on MTV at the time ("Hungry Like the Wolf" and "Girls on Film"). The in-store appearance by the band had been heavily plugged by local radio station WPLJ the preceding week.

It was scheduled to begin at two p.m. that Saturday. As early as six a.m., however, hordes of New York's pop-loving youth began to arrive at the doors of Video Shack for what turned into a mostly futile attempt to see the band. In the beginning, the crowd was well behaved. But when a Sony video crew arrived to take footage, the members of the band were quietly escorted into the store through a rear entrance. Once some of the more observant members of the crowd spotted them through the window, all hell broke loose.

Kids began crawling up the gates covering the store window and were being pressed by the excited crowd behind them. The authorities on hand became frightened at this point that the gates would not be strong enough to hold the crowd. Suddenly it was necessary to call in additional police to help maintain order among the Duran Duran fans before someone got hurt. All told, it took more than 150 midtown police (including mounted police) to keep the crowd under control.

At the height of the near riot, it was necessary for Video Shack to actually close down to quell the mob which was still gathering en masse. Not only were the Duran fans growing in number, but small groups of curious on-lookers were gathering to see what all the excitement was about. Policemen managed to clear the sidewalks eventually, although a pair of mounted police on two very nervous horses caused a brief moment of panic when they tried to clear the entrance to the store.

When the area was finally cleared and things were under control once again, Video Shack raised its iron gates and allowed approximately twenty fans at a time in to be "Duraned," as they say. Once inside, fans were encouraged to buy one of the new Sony 45s after they received autographs and photos and general greetings from the band.

Marcia Kesselman, Video Shack's director of promotion and advertising, reported that nearly two hundred of the Duran video 45s were sold during the hour and forty-five minute in-store session. She also reported that there may have been three injuries suffered by some of the more enthusiastic fans, including one broken foot. That fan was scheduled to receive a personal phone call from the band at a later date to help ease the pain. Parents of the hundred or so fans who did not receive entrance to the store called to complain to the Video Shack manager. Those people later received a special "I was Duran-Duraned at Video Shack" T-shirt which were going to be printed as an extra attraction at the next scheduled Duran Duran in-store appearance.

Despite the scary and potentially dangerous scene, Video Shack, Capitol Records and the Sony Corporation were very pleased with the results of the Duran Duran promotion, and, in fact, plan a ten to twelve city tour of either video or record stores for the band. What was most important, they felt, was that many lessons were learned from the first event. As Bob Janeczek (U.S. operations manager for video software at Sony Consumer Products) told then-*Cashbox* reporter Jim Bessman: "We more or less learned our lesson. We'll need more control through better security, in-store layout and notifying the police in advance. Also, instead of rushing ten people in at a time, we'll have an "S"-shaped lineup with police barricades to funnel people in, instead of mass hysteria." Other plans by authorities include having pictures autographed in advance and then having them be personalized by the band on the spot in order to eliminate the slow and often tedious process by which fans obtained as many as five signatures.

Another interesting suggestion which surfaced after the near riot, was to create a "calming room" to keep fans from jumping and screaming when they finally do get in to meet the band. A nice idea, the calming room would be an area where the more dramatic fans could compose themselves before meeting their idols.

Fortunately, a total riot was averted on this particular occasion. All in all, everyone involved with the promotion was pleased. The promotional and advertising people were happy with the elevated sales and fans were happy to have met the band and gotten their autographs. The event even garnered the attention, by way of camera crews and network coverage, of New York's three networks and one independent news station as well as TV coverage in London.

In the first year that it was on the market the Sony 45 garnered the Record Industry Association of America gold award for having sold over one million copies.

So the next time you see a large, anxious crowd gathered around the midtown area of your town, stop and take a look at what's happening. Maybe Duran Duran is in town.

11. The World According To Duran Duran

To really get to know someone there is no better way than to sit down and talk with them for a while. Needless to say, interviewers from virtually every rock publication around the world today has had the pleasure of talking with Duran Duran (*Rolling Stone*, *Star Hits*, *Rock Magazine*, *Melody Maker*, *New Musical Express* and *The Record*, just to name a few). In doing research for this book, I was struck by the candidness with which Duran Duran conducts an interview, and I honestly felt that I learned more about the band by just reading what they had to say. Therefore, I felt no book about Duran Duran would be complete without some of the more clever and intelligent quotations from band members that I discovered. So here they are, right from the horse's mouth.

"There was one day when we all sat around and realized that nothing can stop us. I didn't think we'd ever break the States though."
> — John Taylor, 1983

"I enjoy life, but most of all I enjoy work."
> — Simon Le Bon, 1983

"It was the first time my eyes welled up in ages. Everyone was ga-ga. We recorded the show and I played like a complete idiot."
> — John Taylor, 1983
> (Referring to a Madison Square Garden
> gig during their 1984 tour)

"Fourteen-year-old girls? I love them — especially after breakfast."
> — John Taylor, 1984

"I've been interested in music since I was twelve. When John got out of art school, we thought it would be great to start a band, even though we didn't play anything."
> — Nick Rhodes, 1984

"I think what we're criticized for most is that we're flaunting our money, like we're saying look at everything we have with the money we make from our records you buy. But that's really not the case at all."
— John Taylor, 1984

"We don't want to be has-beens by the time we're twenty-five. It would be the worst thing in the world to go around saying to people 'Do you know who I used to be?' "
— Roger Taylor, 1983

"A year ago this time, we couldn't have sold eggs in America."
— Andy Taylor, 1984

"That's what people do, they work and have parties. I like parties. I don't think there's anything wrong with that at all."
— Simon Le Bon, 1984

"Maybe we should have worn masks."
— Nick Rhodes, 1984
(When asked if many of the group's fans are attracted to them only for their good looks.)

"We are constantly referred to as a 'teenybopper band.' But you've seen our audiences. I

mean, I wouldn't call that teeny, would you?"
— Simon Le Bon, 1984

"For a band to break out of Birmingham, you've got to be better than if you were from somewhere else. That's the best thing about the place."

— Roger Taylor, 1983

"We have no private life. If you go to a restaurant it's in the paper."

— Roger Taylor, 1983

"I don't think there is anything constructive about marching on the House of Parliament or, you know, breaking down the walls of Babylon. I think we're more in favor of free enterprise."

— John Taylor, 1984

"I think the fairy-tale band image is a nice image. But, the fact is, behind all the good luck and all the nice things that have happened, there has been a great deal of hard work."
— Simon Le Bon, 1982

"If I was rich and wasn't doing this, I'd pay to do it! Just to get up on stage and have all those people *looking* at you."

— Simon Le Bon, 1981

"I feel one of the major reasons for our success is that we don't have times when we lose control of reality. You've just got to keep a karma throughout."

— Nick Rhodes, 1982

'Basically speaking, if you've got something on your mind, you shouldn't give up until you get it."

— Simon Le Bon, 1981

"I suppose it's fabulous. But it's very hit and miss though, it could be over tomorrow."

— Andy Taylor, 1982

"I take video seriously, I see it as an art form. Videos are the talking pictures of today's music industry."

— Simon Le Bon, 1983

"Those two hours on stage are *great*! I love that power. I've always been incredibly shy. I was the kid who would sit in the back of the class. Performing has given me a lot of strength."

— John Taylor, 1984

"Survival is part of our ambition. To survive in this business is a great feat. But it's no good making a great business success if it destroys you as an individual."

— Simon Le Bon, 1983

"It's all of our lives, it's all we've ever wanted to do."

— John Taylor, 1981

12. Duran Duran — Yesterday, Today, Tomorrow (And Forever)

Duran Duran had its humble beginnings in 1978. Today in 1984 they are nothing short of megastars, having captured audiences all around the world with their unique brand of dance romance music. There isn't a pop-loving fan out there who hasn't heard one of their many hit singles on the radio or in a club. Nor is there a record chart in any country that hasn't been graced by a Duran Duran song in its top ten. In six short years Duran Duran have achieved what most other artists cannot do in ten. And this is only the beginning.

Duran Duran is a young band. Except for

Simon Le Bon, all of its members are under twenty-five, and like most great artists and good wine, they have already begun to improve with age. Listen to their very first single, "Planet Earth," and then listen to a more recent cut like "Union of the Snake" or "The Reflex." The masterful changes in musicianship, in production quality and in overall musical maturity are very apparent. The lyrics are more sophisticated, the vocals are sharper and clearer than before—more controlled. The bass and percussion lines have a distinct direction. Also, the *Seven and the Ragged Tiger* LP is full of a spirit of adventure not evident on the two previous LPs. As musician and as a band this quintet is most certainly developing. The very pop aspects of their music are still there but now they are more subtle, more disguised, and consequently the Duran Duran sound is becoming better then ever.

The directions this band could go in are endless. But there is no doubt their first and foremost musical strategy will remain the same—this group wants to make music that people can dance to. Coming of age as the fashionable punk era was coming to a close in England, the Durans simply wanted to make music that would be sheer escapist entertainment—danceable, a lot of fun and very well done. No more heavy political messages through music, no more preaching to the youth of the world. It was time to have a good time.

Duran Duran attempted to dispel much of the pessimism that existed in their British homeland. They wanted to be, and now have become, a positive force in modern music. They have become the perfect example of people who have worked themselves up to very fortunate positions, doing what they want to do most and doing it exactly as they would like. It has always been the desire of all the Durans to carry along this message: It's OK to be an individual, to do what you want with your life. And if you want to, aim for something really big. Unlike the punkers, the Durans did not want to encourage any particular lifestyle. It was more important to convince their audiences that they should believe in who you are and do what you want with your life.

What's most impressive about all of this is that Duran Duran has certainly taken their own advice. When they became unhappy with the new romantic image that was put upon them early in their careers, they were quick to dispense with the ruffles and frilly clothing. They wanted a more sophisticated look and they went after it. Even when they were heavily criticized for making what the critics called "artistically worthless" music, they stuck to their original concepts and continued to make the kind of music they wanted to make. Today they are superstars for their determined efforts. Both the audiences and critics are now coming around to their point of view. All this is very impressive indeed for a band that has only been making music for a little over six years.

In the beginning Duran Duran were most often compared to the Beatles. Many similarities do exist. Both groups hail from small English towns, both were purveyors of a new musical sound and both have had an incredible impact on the world of rock & roll. And like the Beatles, Duran Duran has a tidal wave of young, female followers. When Beatlemania was at its height, the members of Duran Duran were still in diapers. Now the girls who used to faint over John, Paul, George and Ringo have given birth (in some cases literally) to a whole new generation of pop fanatics—the Duranies.

Another important characteristic the Durans share with the Beatles of the 1960s is that no one member totally dominates the group—there really is no leader. Duran Duran function as a group. Each member makes a very important contribution to the whole. Simon is the lyricist and vocalist. John, Nick, Andy and Roger write the music and play it. All have a hand in album production. Every fan has his or her favorite Duran star.

What this amounts to is a total lack of re-sentiment between band members. Although John and Nick can take credit for creating the group, they do not come forward as leaders. Each of the Durans depends on the inventiveness and creativity of the other members to complete the Duran Duran image and sound. There's a great deal of love and respect between these guys. They have survived a great deal together already and they plan on sticking together.

There is a lot to like about Duran Duran. More than likely the characteristic that will immediately attract the masses are the band's sporting and provocative good looks. Yes, they are handsome, but their youth and idealism and self-made success is also a very attractive plus. And of course, their talent goes without saying. But a positive attitude is contagious, especially in these difficult times in our world today. Duran Duran has infected their audiences with a positivism that has not been witnessed for a long time by our contemporary culture. It makes people feel good to know that it is still possible to have a good time and be successful.

Duran Duran is made up of five intelligent young men. Men who have worked hard and furiously to get what they wanted. Men who have risen to the challenges of stardom with grace and maturity well beyond their years. John Cougar Mellencamp stated in an interview recently that he didn't know how a kid of twenty-one could handle success—he didn't see how they could possibly be ready for it. "Imagine a twenty-one-year-old kid being star of the year," he said, "I think it would ruin his life." Well, this is exactly what happened to Duran Duran. They had achieved great success in their homeland as well as in Australia and several other countries and were beginning to attract some attention in America when they were only about twenty years old! Yet they managed to avoid the usual unfavorable traps that often accompany rock & roll stardom: drinking problems, drugs, ego problems, management and business ripoff. They also managed to avert falling into the dilemma of being proverbial "one-hit wonders." Duran Duran did not come and go, like a song, in a flash. Duran Duran came and they stayed.

Longevity is certainly a problem for any band or recording artist. As musical modes and genres develop and change, a musical group can easily go by the wayside and become nothing but a momentary spotlight on a golden oldies program a few years down the line. But Duran Duran seem to be a band with staying power. "We've been through some weird situations," says Simon Le Bon, "and if we've managed to survive them, we'll stick together through everything. This band will last a long time."

It's interesting (but sad) to think of what might happen to Duran Duran if they ever decide to go their separate ways. It *is* an occupational hazard, after all. Many difficulties arise when a rock band has been together for many years. And it isn't always personality conflicts or artistic disagreements. As is the case in all high-powered professions — and especially for artists — people reach plateaus and have to move on.

There are very few bands that have managed to stay together and still make fine music through several decades. The Rolling Stones and the Who (before they, too, broke up) immediately come to mind. But this doesn't seem to be in the air for Duran Duran just yet, though each member of the group certainly has enough talent and ambition to see him through a solo career. Each one knows enough about songwriting and music-making to build an individual career. And it's unlikely that the fans would desert any of the Duran Durans that chose to make it on his own. Their loyalty would remain strong.

The fact is, Duran Duran are very happy together. Artistically they compliment each other very well and all look forward to growing and developing as a musical entity. They have a lot of experimenting to do as musicians. And certainly there is always room for any one member to stretch his wings a little bit and delve into some kind of solo project. Evidence of this is Nick Rhodes' recent work with Kajagoogoo and his photographic endeavors.

Part of the Duran Duran success story has been that this quintet offered a new mode made up not only of their music but also of their style and appeal. They have also used other new trends in rock & roll to their best advantage — video, for example. Nick Rhodes has said that "video is to Duran Duran what stereo was to Pink Floyd." That is, they saw this new promotional tool as something they could do a lot with and decided to take that bull by the horns and use it like no other band before them had done. While other artists were busy making films and videos out of ordinary concert footage, Duran Duran capitalized on the idea of conceptualizing their songs. A Duran Duran video is essentially a mini-movie, with a plot, a star and a concept all enhanced by an unusual locale or setting, not to mention state-of-the-art production work. For those three or four minutes, the Duran Duran fan becomes immersed in a fantasy — a dream date, if you will. And the fans' pleasure is very important to these guys. After all, without their fans, where would they be? And what the fans will do in turn for their idols is equally engaging.

Finding a Duranie glued to a TV set tuned in to MTV is just the beginning of the type of adoration you can find among Duran Duran devotees. Showing up outside the hotel where they are staying while on tour in your town, is carrying things a bit further (how fans manage to uncover that kind of confidential information is baffling). Actually getting into the hotel, or their rooms, or their closets (remember Andy's surprise) takes real determination. These events might sound a bit far-fetched to some, but not to anyone who is a real Duranie. When it comes to these guys the fans leave no stone unturned. But most of you probably already know about the polite sieges that follow the band wherever they can. They've been followed into limousines, into restaurants, into hotels and they've been mobbed at concerts. Many of you reading this book have probably spent endless hours waiting in ticket lines, or behind police barricades in front of a major hotel, or even in an airport waiting for the band's plane to arrive. In short, there isn't much a Duran Duran lover wouldn't do to make contact with any one of these guys.

"I've been hanging out for four or five days, eight or nine hours every day," said one eager fan who had been waiting outside the Berkshire Place hotel when Duran Duran were in New York for their Madison Square Garden gig in

March. "My mother hates this," she continued, "but it really has been great. Not only did I get to meet the band, but I've met a lot of nice people."

Another die-hard Duran Duran watcher said: "Yeah, I did wait a long time, but it was worth it. When they finally arrived at the hotel, they were really nice. Nick smiled at me, I'm sure of it. I couldn't believe they were standing right there in front of me! I could almost touch John, he was that close!"

Yet another ardent fan was surprised by what she saw after attending a Duran Duran concert. "I knew they all wore makeup, but I didn't realize they would be wearing so much. Simon was as good-looking as he is on TV."

Some fans have been more fortunate than others in their efforts to meet the band. *Star Hits* magazine recently conducted a Duran Duran Win-A-Date contest. The six winners were flown to San Francisco to meet the band and attend one of their concerts this summer. The magazine reported having received a mind-boggling 108 thousand entries of all shapes and description, which turned their offices into a virtual obstacle course of paper and mailbags.

When the six lucky winners were notified by phone, the common reaction was first dumb-struck silence, then disbelief (more than one answered with "This is a joke, right?"), then wild, hysterical screaming. None could believe they had really won. None could believe they were really going to meet Duran Duran. When the winners finally got to San Francisco and met the band backstage, these were just some of their general reactions, thoughts and memories:

—"Simon's kiss, it was great. Even though it was on the side of my face, it felt like it went right through to my soul."

—"I'm gonna tell them, 'Hey, I really like your music' . . . then I'll attack them."

—"The kids were screaming so loud you could hear their voices crack. When they do wild things, you just have to scream because they look so gorgeous."

—"I think I said hi to Roger!"

—"I wish I could have felt John's hand. He was wearing those fingerless, red gloves and he was such a ham. I saw him look right into the camera and wave."

—"I'm looking for some serious lip-lock!"

But not everyone is lucky enough to win such a contest. Others must rely on the deluge

151

of rock and pop magazines to hit the news-stands every month in order to keep up with the latest Duran² (as the trades have come to refer to them) news. The Letters to the Editor column has become a stage where Duran Duran fans can unite and share their true feelings about the band. Also, the Letters column has become an arena where true D² fans can defend their idols from the negative press and people who write in letters against the Durans. In an average column you would find letters like these:

—"Duran Duran are my true buds, I would bear their children—no prob!"

—"Calling all proofreaders: WAKE UP! It's Nicholas *James* Bates, not Nicholas John . . . Sheesh!

—"I'm writing to inform you that Duranmania is alive and thriving. To all those who imply that DD is just for screaming girls, find yourself a very tall bridge spanning a shallow river."

—"They are my favorite group because they play good music (though I can't deny they're good looking). So all of you girls who made DD teenybopper idols, stay out of my eyesight and earshot."

—"Dearest Sylvia Rhodes, I'd like to thank you for bringing such a lovely and angelic creature into the world."

For all the love, admiration and loyalty Duran Duran receives from their most ardent fans, they return the courtesy by putting out the best possible records and putting on the best possible shows. Also, being very much aware of just how much their fans want to feel close to them, Duran Duran try to make themselves as accessible as possible through the various sources: industry trades, newspapers and all of the rock-oriented magazines on the market today. Beside the need to keep their fans happy, the Durans also realize the grave responsibility they have toward their mostly young and very impressionable followers. Any kind of bad image the band might put forth might have an unfavorable effect on them. As John Taylor said in a recent interview: "I think it's bad to preach to kids. We've got a young audience at a very impressionable age, and it would be rough on them if we started lecturing. The main responsibility we have is to give people a good time, to give them what they pay for."

But putting yourself under constant public scrutiny is not an easy thing to live with. Although they have done their best to remain constant figures in the eyes of their public, Duran Duran has also managed incredibly to maintain some degree of privacy in their lives. It's been very important to all involved to keep their personal lives, apart from the band, their own business. After all, I don't think there would be anyone who would disagree that even a rock star deserves a private life. Of course not everything can be public knowledge.

Each member of Duran Duran strives to maintain as much normalcy to their lives as possible, without offending their public. Despite hectic touring schedules, promotional responsibilities and the busy days in the recording studio, all of the Durans still enjoy the small pleasures of life: quiet dinners with friends, holidays with families and even things as simple as sitting home and watching television. Of course, they have much less time for all of this than maybe you or I, but this only makes those simple activities that much more enjoyable.

Perhaps this is what makes John, Nick, Andy, Simon and Roger such genuine characters in the eyes of their fans. They have not become caught up in the all-too-common rock star ego trip. This underlying factor probably has a lot more to do with Duran Duran's success than most people allow for. The record-buying public is not insensitive; they can easily recognize and will be quick to turn away from phonies. The five Duran Duran musicians are real, and they are honest. They are a fine example of human willpower and determination taken to its limits—and people like to see that. They have worked incredibly hard to achieve success. Although many of the group's members would be quick to include luck among their success factors, none will deny that it has been a hard climb to the top. John, for example, remembers some of the more difficult times: "We toured bars and clubs, performing on a four-by-five-foot stage and we'd have three people in the audience." But with determination, long hours and very careful planning, Duran Duran made it to the very top of the heap. Each member is proud of his accomplishments, each is proud to have so many people partaking in his dreams.

What does the future hold for Duran Duran? No one, of course, can say for sure, but one thing is certain: Nick, John, Andy, Simon and Roger have already conquered the most difficult part of being celebrities. They have fought for recognition, developed a style and image that comfortably suits them, and put up with the sometimes malicious criticism that haunts virtually every public figure. It may seem that once an entertainer surmounts these obstacles life should be a breeze. But what lies ahead are still many years of hard work. Fame is not so much their concern anymore, but artistic expression and creative development are.

The members of Duran Duran have reached a point where new goals and ambitions must be planned. This not an easy task. But anyone who has followed the band thus far can be confident that Duran Duran have not seen their heyday yet. These mature talents have only just begun to recognize their true potential as musicians and songwriters. From one album to another they are still developing. Music is a rapidly changing vein of artistic expression and Duran Duran have already proven that they are dynamic musicians always looking for new ideas to incorporate into their music. The changing tides are, for them, a vital and creative part of the music industry. They don't face the future with fear but with enthusiasm and excitement.

It's interesting to think of the different fields of entertainment Duran Duran could venture into other than music. Of course, they are musicians at heart, but it would be great to see the Durans do a feature-length film. The Beatles were very successful with their film projects *Help!* and *A Hard Day's Night*. Both have become motion picture classics. With the talent these guys have displayed in front of video cameras, you can be pretty sure they'd be absolutely dynamite in a full-length film.

During their recent concert tour, a film crew from *The Tube* (a rock & roll show broadcast over British TV) did tape segments of Duran Duran's two homecoming shows at the National Exhibition Center in Birmingham, as well as interviews with the band. Although this kind of documentary is a great beginning, what all Duranies look forward to is a real Duran Duran movie. Maybe Duran Duran would even consider doing all the music for a film or writing a concept album that could be made into a film, like *Tommy*, for example.

Television is also an interesting prospect. Many of you may remember the zany half hour TV show the Monkees did in the 1960s which cleverly combined music with situation comedy. What would be more fun than tuning in to a half hour of Duran Duran once a week!

The word is out that Duran Duran fans may not have to wait very long to see the group's talents displayed on the big silver screen. Nick Rhodes has plans to realize his dream of directing films and will be working on a short fantasy adventure film later on in 1984. Nick will be both producer and director of the film. Meanwhile, Simon is very interested in renewing his acting career in between Duran Duran gigs. He made an announcement at the recent

157

Cannes Film Festival that the William Morris public relations agency may soon be handling his acting career. Apparently, Simon has already been deluged with film offers. He has been offered a variety of different roles ranging from British cavalry man to an Elvis Presley type rock & roll idol. So far Simon has not found the exact part that he is looking for, but you can bet it won't be long before he will star in a major motion picture.

Most importantly they will not sit back and wait to see what life will hand them. These are five artists who go after what they want—and get it. Like wide-eyed children on a merry-go-round, Duran Duran are after the ultimate golden ring—and nothing will stop them until they capture it.

Certainly the future will see many more fine albums from this quintet as well as many more hit singles. Performing will probably remain their favorite thing to do, hence much of their time in years to come will be spent honing and developing their already dynamic stage show which they will deliver with great finesse to virtually every country of the world. Regardless of what they do, they will be making their millions of fans very happy. As the years go by and Duran Duran continue to develop as artists they will win over more and more admirers. Already it is difficult for anyone who loves music not to be caught up in the melodic and infectious music of the suave Durans. With songs like "Rio" or "Planet Earth" or "Union of the Snake," tempting the world to get up and dance, you can bet that Duran Duran's following will just keep growing bigger and bigger!

Duran Duran At A Glance

JULY 1980—The completed lineup of Duran Duran consisting of members Simon Le Bon, Nick Rhodes, John Taylor, Andy Taylor and Roger Taylor play their first big concert date together at the Edinburgh Festival.

NOVEMBER 1980—Duran Duran are the opening act for Hazel O'Connor's U.K. tour.

JANUARY 1981—As a result of the live performance with the O'Connor tour, Duran Duran land a record contract with EMI Records.

FEBRUARY 1981—Duran Duran's first single, "Planet Earth," is released. It rises to number twelve on the U.K. charts.

MAY 1981—Duran Duran headline their first tour of the United States.

JUNE 1981—"Planet Earth" is released in the States as a single.

JUNE 1981—The first packaging of the *Duran Duran* LP is released in the U.K. It reaches number two on the U.K. charts.

SEPTEMBER 1981—"Girls on Film" is released as a single in U.K. It reaches number five on the charts. Duran Duran begin to receive airplay in America.

APRIL 1982—Duran Duran play a concert tour in Australia.

MAY 1982—Duran Duran's second LP, *Rio*, is released worldwide. It reaches the number two spot in Britain.

JUNE 1982—The first single off the LP is released: "Hungry Like the Wolf."

JUNE 1982—MTV begins airing the video of "Hungry Like the Wolf." The response is incredible.

JULY 1982—Duran Duran begin a two-month, thirty-four-date concert tour of North America.

JULY 1982—Andy Taylor marries Tracy Wilson in Los Angeles.

SEPTEMBER 1982—Capitol Records releases *Carnival*, a four-song mini-LP.

OCTOBER 1982—"Rio," the title tune from their second LP is released as a single. The song rises to number three on the American charts.

DECEMBER 1982—Duran Duran headline the MTV annual New Year's Eve special.

DECEMBER 1982—The remixed version of "Hungry Like the Wolf" is released and promptly zooms to the number three spot on the American charts.

MARCH 1983—A new single, "Is There Something I Should Know," is released in the U.K. It enters the charts at number one. This is Duran Duran's first number one single.

MARCH 1983—The *Duran Duran* video LP is released, featuring the band's first eleven videos.

MARCH 1983—Duran Duran cause a virtual riot at an in-store appearance at a New York Video Shack.

APRIL 1983—A remixed and repackaged version of the *Duran Duran* LP is released in the States. The album reaches number ten on the charts and sells over one million copies.

MAY 1983—"Is There Something I Should Know" is released as a single in the United States. The song rises to number four.

JULY 1983—Duran Duran headline a performance at the Dominion Theater in England before the Prince and Princess of Wales.

OCTOBER 1983—A first single from a yet-unreleased Duran Duran LP is released. "Union of the Snake" reaches number three in Britain and cracks the top ten in America.

NOVEMBER 1983—Duran Duran release their third LP, *Seven and the Ragged Tiger*. In 1984 the album will go platinum and remain in the American top ten for several months.

NOVEMBER 1983—Duran Duran's third worldwide concert tour begins.

DECEMBER 1983—Duran Duran perform five shows at England's prestigious Wembley Arena.

JANUARY 1984—Duran Duran tour the United States.

JANUARY 1984—A second single from the *Seven and the Ragged Tiger* LP called "New Moon on Monday" is released.

MARCH 1984—Duran Duran perform at New York's Madison Square Garden.

APRIL 1984—A third single, "The Reflex," is released.

The Duran Duran
Discography

THE ALBUMS

Duran Duran (debut LP)
released April, 1983
(ST-1258 Capitol)

"Girls on Film"
"Planet Earth"
"Is There Anyone Out There"
"Careless Memories"
"Is There Something I Should Know"

"(Waiting for the) "Nightboat"
"Sound of Thunder"
"Friends of Mine"
"Tel Aviv"

Rio
released May, 1982
(ST-12211 Capitol)

"My Own Way"
"Lonely in Your Nightmare"
"Hungry Like the Wolf"
"Hold Back the Rain"
"New Religion"
"Last Chance on the Stairway"
"Save a Prayer"
"The Chauffeur"

Seven and the Ragged Tiger
released November, 1983
(ST-12310 Capitol)

"The Reflex"
"New Moon on Monday"
"(I'm Looking for) A Crack in the Pavement"
"I Take the Dice"
"Of Crimes and Passion"
"Union of the Snake"

"Shadows on Your Side"
"Tiger/Tiger"
"The Seventh Stranger"

MINI ALBUM

Carnival
released September, 1982 — now deleted
(DLP-15006 Capitol)

Extended versions of:
"Girls on Film"
"Hungry Like the Wolf"
"Hold Back the Rain"
"My Own Way"

SINGLES

"Planet Earth"
   (released June, 1981)
"Girls On Film"
   (released September, 1981)
"Hungry Like the Wolf"
   (released June, 1982)

"Rio"
   (released October, 1982)
"Hungry Like the Wolf"
(Remixed Night Version)
   (released December, 1982)
"Rio"
(Remixed extended version)
   (released March, 1983)
"Is There Something I Should Know"
   (released May, 1983)
"Union of the Snake"
   (released October, 1983)
"New Moon on Monday"
   (released January, 1984)
"The Reflex"
   (released April, 1984)

TWELVE-INCH SINGLES

"Is There Something I Should Know"
   (released June, 1983)
"Union of the Snake"
   (released October, 1983)
"The Reflex"
   (released April, 1984)

Videography

The Duran Duran Video LP
 released March, 1983

1. "Planet Earth" directed by Russell Mulcahy
2. "Careless Memories" directed by Perry Haines
3. "Girls on Film" by Kevin Godley & Lol Creme
4. "My Own Way" directed by Russell Mulcahy
5. "Hungry Like the Wolf" directed by Russell Mulcahy
6. "Save a Prayer" directed by Russell Mulcahy

7. "Rio" directed by Russell Mulcahy
8. "Lonely in Your Nightmare" directed by Russell Mulcahy
9. "Nightboat" directed by Russell Mulcahy
10. "The Chauffeur" directed by Ian Eames
11. "Is These Something I Should Know" directed by Russell Mulcahy

NEW VIDEOS

"Union of the Snake" directed by Russell Mulcahy
"New Moon on Monday" directed by Russell Mulcahy
"The Reflex" directed by Russell Mulcahy

EXCITING BESTSELLERS FROM ZEBRA

HEIRLOOM   (1200, $3.95)
by Eleanora Brownleigh
The surge of desire Thea felt for Charles was powerful enough to
convince her that, even though they were strangers and their marriage was a fake, fate was playing a most subtle trick on them both:
Were they on a mission for President Teddy Roosevelt—or on a cru-
sade to realize their own passionate desire?

A WOMAN OF THE CENTURY   (1409, $3.95)
by Eleanora Brownleigh
At a time when women were being forced into marriage, Alicia
Turner had achieved a difficult and successful career as a doctor.
Wealthy, sensuous, beautiful, ambitious and determined—Alicia
was every man's challenge and dream. Yet, try as they might, no
man was able to capture her heart—until she met Henry Thorpe,
who was as unattainable as she!

PASSION'S REIGN   (1177, $3.95)
by Karen Harper
Golden-haired Mary Bullen was wealthy, lovely and refined—and
lusty King Henry VIII's prize gem! But her passion for the handsome Lord William Stafford put her at odds with the Royal Court.
Mary and Stafford lived by a lovers' vow: one day they would be
ruled by only the crown of PASSION'S REIGN.

LOVESTONE   (1202, $3.50)
by Deanna James
After just one night of torrid passion and tender need, the dark-
haired, rugged lord could not deny that Moira, with her precious
beauty, was born to be a princess. But how could he grant her freedom when he himself was a prisoner of her love?

*Available wherever paperbacks are sold, or order direct from the
Publisher. Send cover price plus 50¢ per copy for mailing and
handling to Zebra Books, 475 Park Avenue South, New York, N.Y.
10016. DO NOT SEND CASH.*